Hunt's®
Tomato Paste
Recipe
Collection

From the Home Economists
of the
Hunt-Wesson Kitchens

®
Hunt-Wesson Foods, Inc.
Fullerton, California 92634

Contents

Metric Is Coming

The United States will soon be joining in a worldwide effort to standardize all weights and measures by converting to the metric system. Many consumers are apprehensive about the changeover but it will really be quite simple and gradual. We hope this book will help you get a head start in understanding just how easy it will be to make yours a metric kitchen.

Under the Systeme International d'Units, which the U.S. will be using, foods we currently buy by weight, such as meat, pasta and canned foods, will still be sold by weight, but in grams rather than pounds or ounces. To simplify recipe preparation, most ingredients will continue to be measured by volume, but in liters (l) and millileters (ml) rather than cups and teaspoons. Metric "cups" and spoons are becoming available and will be used just as our cup, tablespoon, teaspoon, etc., are now. With these metric measuring tools, metric recipes will be as easy to prepare as your favorite recipes today.

To help you become familiar with the incoming metric system, we've listed the metric measures for ingredients in each recipe. The charts below show equivalents for basic measurements, pan sizes and oven temperatures.

BASIC MEASUREMENTS USED IN COOKING
Abbreviations and Approximate Equivalents

Length — 1 inch = 2.50 centimeters (cm)
Weight — 1 ounce = 28 grams (g)
Volume — 1 cup = 250 millileters (ml)
          1 tablespoon = 15 millileters (ml)
          1 teaspoon = 5 millileters (ml)

Common Pan Sizes	U.S. Customary Units	Metric Units, Rounded
Casseroles	1 quart (qt)	1 liter (l)
	1½ quart (qt)	1.5 liter (l)
	2 quart (qt)	2 liter (l)
Baking Pans	8-inch	20 cm
	9-inch	23 cm
	10-inch tube pan	25 cm
	9 x 13 x 2-inch	23 x 33 x 5 cm
	15½ x 10½ x 1-inch jelly roll pan	39 x 25 x 3 cm
	9 x 5 x 3-inch loaf pan	23 x 13 x 8 cm

Oven Temperatures	°Farenheit (F)	°Celcius (C)
Very slow	250–275	120–135
Slow	300–325	150–165
Moderate	350–375	175–190
Hot	400–425	205–220
Very Hot	450–475	230–245

Note: For convenience, all metric measurements in this book have been rounded off. The resulting dish is in no way changed.

A Good Friend in the Kitchen

Just about everyone loves the taste of tomato. It's the most versatile of flavors, adapting obligingly to many delicious dishes. And tomato paste offers one of the most convenient, economical and easy ways to tomato cookery. Its spooning-thick body makes it cling to all kinds of foods from spaghetti to barbecued chicken. And, because it's a pure concentrate, it enhances dishes with a lively, natural tomato flavor.

This book is Hunt's proud collection of recipes to help you get better acquainted with tomato paste . . . recipes that show what a convenient and compatible companion it can be in all manner of cooking. Of course there are rich, full-flavored homemade sauces to serve over pasta. And there's a whole lot more. Turn the pages to discover good and easy casseroles, delicious meat dishes, marvelous soups and stews. Or find special treats for snacking, interesting ways to dress up vegetables . . . special recipes to try when you're feeling extra creative.

So, do turn an old acquaintance into a good, new friend . . . and, whether you're cooking for family or guests, enjoy the full, rich flavor of tomato paste through the recipes in this book.

Reach for Hunt's Tomato Paste

When You're Thinking of Pasta . . .

In their infinite variety, macaroni, spaghetti and noodles have become a mainstay of everyday cooking in American homes. They form the basis of delightful and economical company dishes, too—everybody loves pasta. Here are recipes for a wide selection of thick, tomato-rich sauces, traditional pasta favorites and tempting new dishes. They're all easy to make and designed with you and your family in mind.

Opposite: Spaghetti with Meatballs (see page

Spaghetti with Meatballs (Illustrated page 7)

Nobody's late for dinner when this is served

	2 eggs, beaten
340 g	2 (6-oz.) or 1 (12-oz.) can Hunt's Tomato Paste
60 ml	¼ cup minced onion
60 ml	¼ cup grated Parmesan cheese
30 ml	2 Tablesp. minced parsley
	1 clove garlic, minced
	Salt
450 g	1 lb. ground beef
180 ml	¾ cup soft bread crumbs
45 ml	3 Tablesp. pure vegetable oil
625 ml	2½ cups hot water
8 ml	1½ teasp. sugar
5 ml	1 teasp. basil
5 ml	1 teasp. oregano
1 ml	¼ teasp. pepper
450 g	1 lb. spaghetti, cooked and drained

In a bowl, mix together eggs, *1 tablespoon* Hunt's Tomato Paste, onion, cheese, parsley, garlic and *1 teaspoon* salt. Add beef and bread crumbs; mix thoroughly. Form into 20 balls, about 1-inch in diameter. Lightly brown in a Dutch oven on all sides in hot oil; drain fat. Blend *remaining* Hunt's Tomato Paste with hot water, sugar, basil, oregano, *1 teaspoon* salt and the pepper in a bowl. Pour over meatballs. Cover, simmer 10 minutes. Uncover, simmer 10 minutes longer. Serve over spaghetti. Makes 6 servings.

For spaghetti that waits 'til you're ready . . . Cook half the regular time in unsalted boiling water with a tablespoon of oil added. Let stand in the hot water until you are ready. Drain; rinse with boiling water; serve immediately.

Spaghetti Caruso

Richly satisfying pasta sauce

225 g	½ lb. chicken livers
170 g	1 (6-oz.) jar artichoke crowns, drained and diced
110 g	1 (4-oz.) can sliced mushrooms, drained
	Butter or margarine
	2 medium onions, minced
170 g	1 (6-oz.) can Hunt's Tomato Paste
500 ml	2 cups water
	1 beef bouillon cube
5 ml	1 teasp. salt
1 ml	¼ teasp. pepper
1 ml	¼ teasp. grated lemon peel
30 ml	2 Tablesp. chopped parsley
450 g	1 lb. spaghetti, cooked and drained

In a skillet, sauté chicken livers, diced artichoke and mushrooms in *2 tablespoons* butter until livers lose redness; chop livers coarsely with edge of cooking spoon. Add onions, *2 more tablespoons* butter and cook until softened, stirring occasionally. Stir in Hunt's Tomato Paste, water, bouillon cube, salt, pepper, lemon peel and parsley. Cover; simmer 10 to 15 minutes, stirring frequently. Serve on hot cooked spaghetti. Makes 6 servings.

Farfalle with Zucchini

Delicious pasta side dish

750 ml	3 cups sliced zucchini
	1 medium onion, chopped
30 ml	2 Tablesp. chopped parsley
15 ml	1 Tablesp. pure vegetable oil
	Butter or margarine
5 ml	1 teasp. salt
	Dash pepper
500 ml	2 cups water
170 g	1 (6-oz.) can Hunt's Tomato Paste
284 g	10 ozs. farfalle or egg noodle bows
	Grated Parmesan cheese

In a skillet, sauté zucchini, onion and parsley in oil and *2 tablespoons* butter; add salt and pepper. In a bowl, mix water with Hunt's Tomato Paste, add to skillet; simmer, covered, about 10 minutes or until zucchini is tender. Cook farfalle or other pasta according to package directions. Add *2 tablespoons* butter; toss to coat. Add zucchini mixture and toss to mix. Serve hot with grated Parmesan. Makes 4 to 6 servings.

Olive Spaghetti with Italian Meat Sauce

Ripe olives add flavor and texture to the pasta

225 g	½ lb. ground beef
250 ml	1 cup chopped onion
	1 clove garlic, minced
340 g	2 (6-oz.) or 1 (12-oz.) can Hunt's Tomato Paste
500 ml	2 cups water
5 ml	1 teasp. salt
3 ml	½ teasp. oregano
3 ml	½ teasp. thyme
1 ml	¼ teasp. pepper
110 g	1 (4-oz.) can sliced mushrooms, undrained
340 g	12 ozs. spaghetti, cooked and drained
130 g	1 (4½-oz.) can sliced ripe olives
	Grated Parmesan cheese

In a skillet, brown beef; add onion and garlic and cook until transparent; drain fat. Stir in Hunt's Tomato Paste, water, seasonings and mushrooms with liquid. Simmer, uncovered, 15 to 20 minutes or until sauce reaches desired consistency; stir occasionally. On heated serving platter, toss hot spaghetti with olives; pour sauce over. Pass cheese. Makes 4 to 6 servings.

Macaroni Salad

It threatens to make potato salad take a back seat

450 g	1 lb. salad macaroni
125 ml	½ cup chopped onion
125 ml	½ cup chopped celery
180 ml	¾ cup sweet pickle relish, undrained
56 g	1 (2-oz.) jar pimientos, chopped
125 ml	½ cup mayonnaise or salad dressing
30 ml	2 Tablesp. Hunt's Tomato Paste
15 ml	1 Tablesp. prepared mustard
10 ml	2 teasp. salt
	2 hard-cooked eggs, chopped
	Paprika

Cook salad macaroni according to package directions; drain and set aside. Meanwhile, combine all remaining ingredients in large mixing bowl; mix thoroughly. Add macaroni; blend well. Chill several hours or overnight. Sprinkle with paprika just before serving. Makes 8 servings.

Red Clam Sauce and Linguine

Traditional – and wonderful – Italian pasta specialty

|--------|--|
	1 onion, chopped
	1 clove garlic, minced
30 ml	2 Tablesp. olive oil
370 g	2 (6½-oz.) cans minced clams, drained
170 g	1 (6-oz.) can Hunt's Tomato Paste
250 ml	1 cup water
30 ml	2 Tablesp. lemon juice
15 ml	1 Tablesp. chopped fresh parsley
5 ml	1 teasp. sugar
1 ml	¼ teasp. rosemary
1 ml	¼ teasp. ground thyme
225 g	8 ozs. linguine or spaghetti, cooked and drained
	Grated Parmesan cheese (optional)

Sauté onion and garlic in oil in skillet. Add clams and their juice, Hunt's Tomato Paste, water, lemon juice, parsley, sugar, rosemary and thyme. Simmer, uncovered, 15 minutes. Serve over cooked linguine; sprinkle with Parmesan, if desired. Makes 4 servings.

For extra flavor in your sauces . . . Use broth, bouillon, beer or wine in place of all or part of the water the recipe calls for.

20-Minute Real Spaghetti Sauce

Little time and effort, lots of rich tomato flavor

125 ml	½ cup chopped onion
	1 clove garlic, crushed
30 ml	2 Tablesp. pure vegetable oil
340 g	2 (6-oz.) or 1 (12-oz.) can Hunt's Tomato Paste
750 ml	3 cups water OR: 1 (14½-oz.) can Hunt's Whole Tomatoes plus 1 cup water
	1 beef bouillon cube
15 ml	1 Tablesp. grated Parmesan cheese
15 ml	1 Tablesp. sugar
3 ml	½ teasp. <u>each</u>: basil, oregano and salt
.5 ml	⅛ teasp. pepper

In a heavy 1½-quart saucepan, sauté onion and garlic in oil until tender. Add remaining ingredients; mix thoroughly. Simmer, covered, 15 minutes, stirring occasionally. Serve over spaghetti or favorite pasta; sprinkle with additional grated Parmesan cheese, if desired. Makes (about 1 quart) 6 to 8 servings.

Old-Country Pot Roast and Spaghetti

A tradition in many families

30 ml	2	Tablesp. pure vegetable oil
900 g	2	lb. chuck roast (about 2 in. thick)
	1	small onion, chopped
	1	clove garlic, minced
10 ml	2	teasp. oregano
5 ml	1	teasp. thyme
5 ml	1	teasp. salt
3 ml	½	teasp. basil
1 ml	¼	teasp. pepper
.5 ml	⅛	teasp. cinnamon
170 g	1	(6-oz.) can Hunt's Tomato Paste
875 ml	3½	cups water
450 g	1	lb. spaghetti
		Grated Parmesan or Romano cheese

Heat oil in large kettle. Brown meat slowly on all sides. Remove meat and lower heat; add onion, garlic and seasonings. Cook gently about 5 minutes. Return meat. Mix Hunt's Tomato Paste with water, pour over meat. Bring to full boil; lower heat. Cover; simmer slowly about 1½ hours, turning meat occasionally. When meat is tender and sauce thickened, cook spaghetti. Slice meat; serve alongside spaghetti; top with sauce and grated cheese. Makes about 6 servings.

Sausage Noodle Ring

Impressive enough for company

225 g	½	lb. bulk pork sausage
220 g	8	ozs. egg noodles
284 g	1	(10-oz.) pkg. frozen chopped spinach, partially thawed
	3	eggs
375 ml	1½	cups milk
170 g	1	(6-oz.) can Hunt's Tomato Paste
5 ml	1	teasp. salt
35 g	1	(1¼-oz.) env. cheese sauce mix
30 ml	2	Tablesp. drained pickle relish

In a large skillet, cook sausage until brown and crumbly; drain; set aside. Meanwhile, cook noodles in boiling salted water 5 minutes. Add spinach; cook 5 to 10 minutes longer or until noodles are tender; drain. In a bowl, lightly beat together eggs, milk, Hunt's Tomato Paste and salt. Add noodles, spinach and cooked sausage and toss lightly. Spoon into well-greased 8-cup ring mold (or 9-inch square pan). Bake at 350°F 25 to 30 minutes until knife inserted in center comes out clean. Prepare cheese sauce mix according to package directions; stir in pickle relish. Serve over noodle ring. Makes 6 to 8 servings.

osite: *Potpourri of Pasta*

Minestrone

Sturdy, more than a soup favorite

500 ml	2	cups chopped onion
250 ml	1	cup chopped celery
60 ml	¼	cup chopped parsley
	1	clove garlic, minced
60 ml	¼	cup pure vegetable oil
170 g	1	(6-oz.) can Hunt's Tomato Paste
298 g	1	(10½-oz.) can beef broth
2250 ml	9	cups water
250 ml	1	cup coarsley chopped cabbage
	2	carrots, thinly sliced
15 ml	1	Tablesp. salt
1 ml	¼	teasp. pepper
1 ml	¼	teasp. sage
450 g	1	(1-lb.) can kidney beans, undrained
	1	zucchini squash, thinly sliced
250 ml	1	cup frozen green beans or peas
250 ml	1	cup alphabet macaroni
		Grated Parmesan cheese

In a large pot, sauté onion, celery, parsley and garlic in oil until soft. Stir in Hunt's Tomato Paste and *next* 7 ingredients. Stir and bring to boil. Lower heat, cover and simmer 1 hour. Add kidney beans and remaining ingredients *except* cheese. Cook 8 to 10 minutes longer or until macaroni is tender. Serve topped with grated Parmesan. Makes 8 to 10 servings

Chili-etti

Old friends meet for a great-flavor get-together

500 ml	2	cups cubed cooked beef
	1	onion, chopped
30 ml	2	Tablesp. pure vegetable oil
170 g	1	(6-oz.) can Hunt's Tomato Paste
450 g	1	(1-lb.) can kidney beans, undrained
500 ml	2	cups water
110 g	4	ozs. spaghetti, broken in 2-inch pieces
5 ml	1	teasp. chili powder
5 ml	1	teasp. salt
250 ml	1	cup shredded Cheddar cheese

Sauté beef and onion in oil in large skillet or Dutch oven; drain fat. Add Hunt's Tomato Paste, kidney beans, water, spaghetti, chili powder and salt. Cover; simmer 12 to 15 minutes or until spaghetti is tender. Stir in cheese; heat just until cheese melts. Makes 4 to 5 servings.

Mostaccioli Milano

An elegant way to serve economical chicken

	2 carrots, thinly sliced
	1 clove garlic, crushed
125 ml	½ cup sliced celery
125 ml	½ cup chopped onion
45 ml	3 Tablesp. minced parsley
30 ml	2 Tablesp. pure vegetable oil
250 ml	1 cup diced cooked chicken
340 g	2 (6-oz.) or 1 (12-oz.) can Hunt's Tomato Paste
500 ml	2 cups water
55 g	1 (2-oz.) can sliced mushrooms, undrained
30 ml	2 Tablesp. white wine
5 ml	1 teasp. salt
225 g	8 ozs. mostaccioli, cooked and drained
	Grated Parmesan cheese

Sauté carrots, garlic, celery, onion and parsley in oil in 10-inch skillet. Add chicken, Hunt's Tomato Paste, water, mushrooms, wine and salt. Bring to boil. Cover; simmer 20 to 25 minutes. Stir occasionally. Spoon over mostaccioli. Sprinkle with Parmesan. Makes 4 to 5 servings.

Spaghettini Bolognese

A classic dish fit for a king

110 g	¼ lb. mushrooms, sliced
	1 carrot, sliced
	1 clove garlic, crushed
125 ml	½ cup each: chopped onion, celery and green pepper
30 ml	2 Tablesp. pure vegetable oil
340 g	¾ lb. Italian sausage, casings removed
340 g	2 (6-oz.) or 1 (12-oz.) can Hunt's Tomato Paste
750 ml	3 cups water
60 ml	¼ cup dry red wine (optional)
5 ml	1 teasp. sugar
1 ml	¼ teasp. Italian herb seasoning
450 g	1 lb. spaghettini, cooked and drained

Sauté mushrooms, carrot, garlic, onion, celery and green pepper in oil in Dutch oven. Add sausage; cook until sausage loses redness; drain fat. Add remaining ingredients except spaghettini. Simmer, uncovered, 30 to 40 minutes, stirring occasionally. Serve over hot cooked spaghettini. Makes 6 to 8 servings.

Macaroni and Beef Casserole

Quick/easy supper—sausage adds zip to the meat sauce

225 g	½	lb. <u>each:</u> lean ground beef and bulk pork sausage
	1	medium onion, chopped
170 g	1	(6-oz.) can Hunt's Tomato Paste
250 ml	1	cup water
3 ml	½	teasp. oregano
3 ml	½	teasp. salt
1000 ml	4	cups cooked elbow macaroni
250 ml	1	cup shredded sharp Cheddar cheese

In a 10-inch skillet, brown beef, sausage and onion; drain fat. Add Hunt's Tomato Paste, water, oregano and salt; simmer 5 minutes. In a 2½-quart casserole layer *half* the macaroni, *half* the meat sauce and *half* the cheese. Repeat layers using *remaining* macaroni, meat sauce and cheese. Bake at 375°F 20 to 25 minutes. Makes 6 servings.

Manicotti Magnifico

If you've never made manicotti, this is the dish to try

	8	manicotti shells
284 g	1	(10-oz.) pkg. frozen, chopped spinach, thawed
250 ml	1	cup ricotta
	2	eggs, slightly beaten
60 ml	¼	cup minced onion
4 ml	¾	teasp. salt
		Dash nutmeg
125 ml	½	cup grated Parmesan cheese
170 g	1	(6-oz.) can Hunt's Tomato Paste
250 ml	1	cup water
60 ml	¼	cup white wine (optional)
	1	clove garlic, crushed
5 ml	1	teasp. sugar
3 ml	½	teasp. Italian herb seasoning

Cook manicotti shells as package directs. Press excess liquid from spinach. In a bowl, combine spinach, ricotta, eggs, onion, salt, nutmeg and *half* the Parmesan; mix well. Fill manicotti shells with mixture. Place in shallow 2-quart baking dish. Combine remaining ingredients *except* Parmesan in a bowl; blend well. Pour over shells. Sprinkle with *remaining* Parmesan. Bake, uncovered, at 375°F 30 to 35 minutes. Makes 4 servings.

Family Recipe Lasagne

Your family will ask for it often

450 g	1	lb. ground beef
	1	medium onion, chopped
	1	clove garlic, minced
5 ml	1	teasp. salt
1 ml	¼	teasp. pepper
3 ml	½	teasp. rosemary (optional)
340 g	2	(6-oz.) or 1 (12-oz.) can Hunt's Tomato Paste
375 ml	1½	cups hot water
225 g	8	ozs. lasagne noodles, cooked and drained
225 g	8	ozs. ricotta or cottage cheese
225 g	8	ozs. mozzarella cheese, sliced
60 ml	¼	cup Parmesan cheese

Cook ground beef, onion and garlic in heavy skillet until beef is crumbly; drain fat. Mix in seasonings, Hunt's Tomato Paste and hot water. Simmer 5 minutes. In a 9 × 13 × 2-inch baking dish, put a thin layer of sauce, *half* the noodles, *all* of the ricotta and *half* of the mozzarella cheese. Repeat with *half* the *remaining* sauce, the noodles, remainder of sauce and mozzarella on top. Sprinkle with Parmesan. Bake at 350°F 30 minutes, or until sauce is bubbling. Let stand 10 minutes before cutting into squares. Makes 6 to 8 servings.

Mushroom-Sauced Spaghetti

Budget-wise meatless main dish

125 ml	½	cup finely chopped onion
30 ml	2	Tablesp. minced carrot
30 ml	2	Tablesp. minced parsley
225 g	½	lb. or 2 (4-oz.) cans mushrooms, sliced
60 ml	¼	cup pure vegetable oil
170 g	1	(6-oz.) can Hunt's Tomato Paste
500 ml	2	cups water
3 ml	½	teasp. salt
3 ml	½	teasp. sugar
225 g	8	ozs. spaghetti, cooked and drained
45 ml	3	Tablesp. melted butter
45 ml	3	Tablesp. grated Parmesan cheese

In a skillet, cook onion, carrot, parsley and mushrooms in hot oil until onion is soft. Stir in Hunt's Tomato Paste, water and seasonings. Simmer, uncovered, 20 minutes. Toss hot cooked spaghetti with melted butter and grated cheese. Top with mushroom sauce. Makes 4 servings.

Fettucine Romano

A famous Italian favorite

225 g	8	ozs. fettucine or wide egg noodles
		Boiling salted water
125 ml	½	cup finely chopped onion
60 ml	¼	cup butter
170 g	1	(6-oz.) can Hunt's Tomato Paste
500 ml	2	cups water
60 ml	¼	cup grated Romano or Parmesan cheese
125 ml	½	cup sour cream
60 ml	¼	cup chopped fresh parsley

Cook fettucine in boiling, salted water until tender; drain well. Meanwhile, sauté onion in butter. Thoroughly blend in Hunt's Tomato Paste and water; heat through. Pour over hot cooked fettucine and toss with Romano cheese. Fold in sour cream. Sprinkle with parsley. Makes 4 to 6 servings.

When you add sour cream . . . Let it come to room temperature. Add just before serving and be sure it doesn't boil.

Pork Chop Noodle Dinner

Sour cream dresses up this easy dinner

	6	pork chops, ½ inch thick
30 ml	2	Tablesp. pure vegetable oil
5 ml	1	teasp. salt
1 ml	¼	teasp. pepper
170 g	1	(6-oz.) can Hunt's Tomato Paste
250 ml	1	cup water
	1	onion, diced
	1	clove garlic, crushed
5 ml	1	teasp. oregano
340 g	1	(12-oz.) pkg. Dutch or extra-wide noodles, cooked and drained
10 ml	2	teasp. poppy seeds or minced parsley
60 ml	¼	cup sour cream

In a large skillet, brown pork chops in hot oil; drain fat. Sprinkle with salt and pepper. Meanwhile, in a bowl, combine Hunt's Tomato Paste, water, onion, garlic and oregano; pour over pork chops. Cover; simmer 30 to 35 minutes or until chops are done. On platter, toss hot noodles with poppy seeds or parsley. Arrange pork chops on top; pour sauce over. Top each chop with spoonful of sour cream. Makes 6 servings.

Reach for Hunt's Tomato Paste

When You Want a Hearty Soup or Stew . . .

They have hit-the-spot appeal because of the great through-and-through flavor that comes from cooking over low heat. Here are soups and stews and some fantastic dishes that incorporate the best of both—you may not know whether to call them soup or stew, but you're sure to call them delicious. Cook your way through a world tour of taste delights, some of them homestyle American—some of them from such far-off places as Spain, France and Germany—some of them courtesy of our South-of-the-Border neighbor.

Opposite: Seafood Gumbo (see page

Seafood Gumbo (Illustrated page 21)

A feast for seafood lovers

	1 clove garlic, minced
	1 large onion, chopped
	½ green pepper, diced
60 ml	¼ cup pure vegetable oil
410 g	1 (14½-oz.) can Hunt's Whole Tomatoes
170 g	1 (6-oz.) can Hunt's Tomato Paste
750 ml	3 cups water
15 ml	1 Tablesp. Worcestershire
10 ml	2 teasp. salt
	1 bay leaf
3 ml	½ teasp. chili powder
3 ml	½ teasp. crushed basil leaves
225 g	½ lb. crab meat
225 g	½ lb. raw shrimp, shelled and cleaned
225 g	½ lb. fresh haddock or halibut, cut in chunks
284 g	1 (10-oz.) pkg. frozen sliced okra, partially thawed
750 ml	3 cups hot cooked rice

In a Dutch oven, sauté garlic, onion and green pepper in oil, stirring until tender. Add *remaining* ingredients *except* seafood, okra and rice. Simmer, uncovered, 45 minutes; remove bay leaf. Add crab, shrimp, haddock and okra; cover and simmer 10 to 12 minutes. Serve in soup bowls over rice. Makes 8 servings.

20-Minute Vegetable Soup

Perfect as a first course or for a luncheon entrée

170 g	1 (6-oz.) can Hunt's Tomato Paste
2000 ml	8 cups water
410 g	1 (14½-oz.) can Hunt's Whole Tomatoes
284 g	1 (10-oz.) pkg. frozen peas
	1 small zucchini, cut in ¼-inch pieces
125 ml	½ cup minced onion
125 ml	½ cup diced celery
125 ml	½ cup finely chopped carrots
	2 vegetable bouillon cubes
	1 bay leaf
10 ml	2 teasp. salt

In a Dutch oven, combine all ingredients. Bring to boil; simmer, covered, 20 minutes. Remove bay leaf. Makes 3 quarts.

Gazpacho

Spain's great gift to soup lovers

410 g	1	(14½-oz.) can Hunt's Whole Tomatoes
170 g	1	(6-oz.) can Hunt's Tomato Paste
375 ml	1½	cups water
	1	medium cucumber, diced
	1	clove garlic, minced
	½	medium green pepper, diced
30 ml	2	Tablesp. pure vegetable oil
30 ml	2	Tablesp. white vinegar
15 ml	1	Tablesp. chopped pimientos
3 ml	½	teasp. salt
3 ml	½	teasp. seasoned salt
3 ml	½	teasp. sugar
1 ml	¼	teasp. Tabasco

In a blender container, combine all ingredients; blend on low speed. Chill at least 2 hours. Makes 6 to 8 servings.

Brunswick Stew

A Southern specialty

	2	slices bacon
1350 g	2½	to 3 lbs. frying chicken pieces
	1	onion, thinly sliced
	1	clove garlic, minced
170 g	1	(6-oz.) can Hunt's Tomato Paste
180 ml	¾	cup water
15 ml	1	Tablesp. sugar
5 ml	1	teasp. Worcestershire
5 ml	1	teasp. salt
1 ml	¼	teasp. pepper
284 g	1	(10-oz.) pkg. frozen whole kernel corn
284 g	1	(10-oz.) pkg. frozen lima beans

In a 12-inch skillet, cook bacon until crisp; remove, crumble and reserve. Pour off all but 2 *tablespoons* drippings. Brown chicken in drippings; add onion and garlic and cook until soft. Stir in Hunt's Tomato Paste, water, sugar, Worcestershire, salt and pepper. Cover; simmer 15 minutes. Add vegetables. Simmer 35 to 40 minutes longer or until lima beans are tender, stirring occasionally. Garnish with reserved crumbled bacon. Makes 4 servings.

To improve canned soups . . . Give canned soups a homemade touch by adding a few tablespoons of tomato paste.

Hearty Beef-Vegetable Soup

Satisfying, easy-do main-dish soup

900 g	2	lbs. stewing beef, cut into 1-inch pieces
1500 ml	6	cups hot water
125 ml	½	cup chopped onion
170 g	1	(6-oz.) can Hunt's Tomato Paste
10 ml	2	teasp. salt
5 ml	1	teasp. ground allspice
1 ml	¼	teasp. thyme
1 ml	¼	teasp. coarsely ground pepper
	2	beef bouillon cubes
	1	bay leaf
	3	carrots, sliced ¼ inch thick
	3	ribs celery, sliced ¼ inch thick
	3	zucchini, sliced ½ inch thick
	2	potatoes, quartered
	¼	head cabbage, cut in 1-inch pieces

Combine *first 10* ingredients in a Dutch oven or large kettle. Bring to boil; simmer, covered, about 2 hours or until meat is tender. Remove bay leaf. Add carrots and *remaining* ingredients. Simmer, covered, 30 minutes longer or until vegetables are tender. Makes 6 to 8 servings.

Bouillabaisse

Simple version of French seafood stew

	1	medium onion, chopped
	1	clove garlic, crushed
30 ml	2	Tablesp. pure vegetable oil
170 g	1	(6-oz.) can Hunt's Tomato Paste
1000 ml	4	cups water
125 ml	½	cup white wine
3 ml	½	teasp. salt
3 ml	½	teasp. fennel seeds
	3	peppercorns
	1	bay leaf
225 g	8	ozs. cooked or canned crab
225 g	8	ozs. cooked or canned shrimp
185 g	1	(6½-oz.) can minced clams, undrained

In a 2½-quart saucepan, sauté onion and garlic in oil until soft. Add *next 7* ingredients; simmer, uncovered, 40 minutes, stirring frequently; remove bay leaf. Add seafood; simmer 5 minutes longer. Makes 4 to 6 servings.

Quick Tomato Rice Soup

Tasty lunchtime treat

625 ml	2½	cups water
170 g	1	(6-oz.) can Hunt's Tomato Paste
15 ml	1	Tablesp. instant chicken bouillon
15 ml	1	Tablesp. butter
10 ml	2	teasp. lemon juice
3 ml	½	teasp. seasoned salt
1 ml	¼	teasp. sugar
	1	bay leaf
60 ml	¼	cup quick-cooking rice

In a 1½-quart saucepan, combine all ingredients *except* rice. Bring to a boil. Add rice; cover and remove from heat. Let stand 7 minutes. Remove bay leaf. Makes 4 servings.

Pork Stew, German Style

A wonderful one-dish meal

900 g	2	lbs. pork shoulder, cut in 1-inch cubes
30 ml	2	Tablesp. pure vegetable oil
5 ml	1	teasp. salt
1 ml	¼	teasp. white pepper
	2	onions, chopped
15 ml	1	Tablesp. paprika
560 ml	2¼	cups water
170 g	1	(6-oz.) can Hunt's Tomato Paste
	2	cloves garlic, minced
	3	medium potatoes, cut in ½-inch-thick slices
450 g	1	(1-lb.) can sauerkraut, drained
15 ml	2 to 3	teasp. caraway seeds

Brown meat in oil in 12-inch skillet; sprinkle with salt and pepper. Add onion and paprika; cook until onion is soft; drain fat. Add water, Hunt's Tomato Paste and garlic; mix well. Cover; simmer 25 minutes. Add remaining ingredients; mix well. Cover; simmer 1 hour longer. Makes 6 to 8 servings.

To prepare in a slow cooker . . . Combine all ingredients except oil in cooker container. Mix thoroughly. Slow cook 6 to 8 hours.

Hungarian Bean Soup

Sour cream blends the flavors, adds mellow tang

225 g	½ lb. small white beans
	Water
	1 small onion, chopped
	2 carrots, sliced
	1 large ham hock
5 ml	1 teasp. salt
1 ml	¼ teasp. pepper
1 ml	¼ teasp. sugar
	1 bay leaf
170 g	1 (6-oz.) can Hunt's Tomato Paste
60 ml	¼ cup sour cream

Wash beans and soak in *4 cups* water in Dutch oven overnight. Drain beans and measure liquid; add enough water to make *4 cups*. Add to beans with onion, carrots, ham hock and seasonings. Bring to boil; simmer, covered, 2 hours. Remove bay leaf and ham. Discard bay leaf and bone; cut up meat and return to soup. Stir in Hunt's Tomato Paste; simmer 10 minutes longer. Mix sour cream and ½ cup hot soup in small bowl; stir; return back into soup gradually. Makes 6 to 8 servings.

Tortilla Soup

	4 corn tortillas
	1 medium onion, finely chopped
	2 cloves garlic, minced
30 ml	2 Tablesp. pure vegetable oil
170 g	1 (6-oz.) can Hunt's Tomato Paste
1125 ml	4½ cups water
180 ml	¾ cup diced cooked chicken
15 ml	3 teasp. instant chicken bouillon
30 ml	2 Tablesp. chopped parsley
10 ml	2 teasp. chili powder
5 ml	1 teasp. salt
	Grated Parmesan cheese

Cut tortillas in ½-inch strips with scissors; set aside (about 30 minutes) to dry. Sauté tortilla strips, onion and garlic in oil in Dutch oven or heavy kettle until onion is soft. Stir in Hunt's Tomato Paste and water. Add chicken, instant bouillon, parsley, chili powder and salt. Simmer 10 to 15 minutes; stir occasionally. Top each serving with generous sprinkling of Parmesan. Makes 6 servings.

Kapama

Greek beef stew with macaroni

675 g	1½	lbs. lean stewing beef, cut in 1-inch pieces
250 ml	1	cup chopped onion
	1	clove garlic, minced
45 ml	3	Tablesp. pure vegetable oil
170 g	1	(6-oz.) can Hunt's Tomato Paste
375 ml	1½	cups water
250 ml	1	cup thinly sliced carrots
60 ml	¼	cup dry red wine (optional)
45 ml	3	Tablesp. minced parsley
3 ml	½	teasp. salt
1 ml	¼	teasp. pepper
625 ml	2½	cups large corkscrew macaroni
250 ml	1	cup shredded Cheddar cheese
60 ml	¼	cup butter or magarine

In a Dutch oven or heavy kettle, cook beef, onion and garlic in oil until beef loses its redness. Stir in *next* 7 ingredients; cover and simmer 1 hour, stirring occasionally. Cook macaroni as package directs; drain. Toss hot cooked macaroni with cheese and butter. Arrange on large serving platter. Spoon meat mixture over macaroni. Makes 6 servings.

Chili Stewpot

Unique variation from the southwest

900 g	2	lbs. round steak, cut in 1-inch cubes
250 ml	1	cup water
250 ml	1	cup chopped onion
410 g	1	(14½-oz.) can Hunt's Whole Tomatoes
	½	green pepper, chopped
5 ml	1	teasp. garlic salt
	2	beef bouillon cubes
110 g	1	(4-oz.) can diced green chilies
450 g	1	(16-oz.) can chili beans, undrained
450 g	1	(16-oz.) can yellow hominy, drained
170 g	1	(6-oz.) can Hunt's Tomato Paste

In a Dutch oven, combine *first* 8 ingredients; stir to mix. Simmer, covered, 1½ hours. Stir once or twice. Add beans, hominy and Hunt's Tomato Paste; mix thoroughly; simmer 30 minutes longer. Makes (about 3 quarts) 8 to 10 servings.

Opposite: Ka

Meatball Soup

Hits-the-spot supper

675 g	1½ lbs. ground beef
	1 egg
125 ml	½ cup soft bread crumbs
125 ml	½ cup water
5 ml	1 teasp. salt
5 ml	1 teasp. dill weed
30 ml	2 Tablesp. pure vegetable oil
1000 ml	1 qt. water
	1 onion, quartered
250 ml	1 cup sliced celery
	1 bay leaf
250 ml	1 cup sliced carrots
170 g	1 (6-oz.) can Hunt's Tomato Paste
5 ml	1 teasp. salt
440 g	1 (15½-oz.) can small red beans or kidney beans, undrained

Combine *first* 6 ingredients; shape into small balls. Brown in oil in deep kettle; drain fat. Add *remaining* ingredients *except* beans. Bring to boil; simmer, covered, 25 minutes. Remove bay leaf and add beans; simmer 10 minutes longer. Makes 6 servings.

French Onion Madrilène

Packaged mix makes it quick

170 g	1 (6-oz.) can Hunt's Tomato Paste
1250 ml	5 cups water
	2 beef bouillon cubes
	1 env. onion soup mix
	4 slices sourdough bread
	Butter
	Parmesan cheese

In a medium saucepan, combine Hunt's Tomato Paste, water, bouillon cube and soup mix. Bring to boil; simmer 5 minutes. Meanwhile, butter bread slices; sprinkle with Parmesan cheese. Place under broiler until cheese melts. Cut into quarters and float in bowls of soup. Makes (6 cups) 6 to 8 servings.

When you have extra tomato paste ... Freeze the tomato paste in 1 or 2 tablespoon portions on wax paper. When frozen, wrap and save for use in soups, gravy, etc.

Manhattan Clam Chowder

Regional favorite for chowder lovers

	4 slices bacon, cut into ½-inch pieces
125 ml	½ cup chopped onion
125 ml	½ cup diced celery
750 ml	3 cups water
250 ml	1 cup diced potatoes
	1 carrot, diced
5 ml	1 teasp. salt
170 g	1 (6-oz.) can Hunt's Tomato Paste
225 g	1 (8-oz.) can minced clams, undrained
1 ml	¼ teasp. ground thyme
.5 ml	⅛ teasp. coarsely ground black pepper

In a 3-quart saucepan, brown bacon until crisp. Add onion and celery; sauté until onion is soft. Drain fat. Add *remaining* ingredients; cover; simmer 20 minutes. Makes 4 (1-cup) servings.

Easy Oven Stew

The oven does the pot-watching for you

60 ml	¼ cup flour
8 ml	1½ teasp. seasoned salt
1 ml	¼ teasp. pepper
1 ml	¼ teasp. paprika
900 g	2 lbs. beef, cut into 1½-inch cubes
30 ml	2 Tablesp. pure vegetable oil
	4 small onions, quartered
	4 small carrots, cut into 1-inch pieces
	4 small potatoes, pared and halved
250 ml	1 cup sliced celery
250 ml	1 cup water
340 g	2 (6-oz.) or 1 (12-oz.) can Hunt's Tomato Paste
8 ml	1½ teasp. salt

Combine flour, seasoned salt, pepper and paprika in plastic bag. Drop in beef, a portion at a time; shake until coated. Mix with oil in 3-quart casserole. Bake, uncovered, at 400°F 30 minutes, stirring once. Add vegetables, water, Hunt's Tomato Paste and salt. Mix well. Cover; bake at 350°F 1 hour 45 minutes or until done. Makes 6 to 8 servings.

Reach for Hunt's Tomato Paste

When You Need a Better Casserole . . .

These are some of Hunt's best. Their happy-
blending secret is tomato paste to point up
the separate flavors and mingle them into a
delectable whole. Rice, pasta, potatoes or
barley go with meat, chicken, fish, cheese and
vegetables in wide, easy-to-make variety. You'll
produce a can't-miss main dish that will do you
proud, that will have the family passing their
plates for seconds.

Opposite: Frankfurter Crowns (see pag

Frankfurter Crowns (Illustrated page 33)

Attractive individual casseroles

535 g	1 (1-lb. 3-oz.) can baked beans
60 ml	¼ cup Hunt's Tomato Paste
30 ml	2 Tablesp. brown sugar, packed
10 ml	2 teasp. instant minced onion
3 ml	½ teasp. dry mustard
450 g	1 (1-lb.) can Boston brown bread
450 g	1 lb. frankfurters
	1 cooking apple (Pippin, McIntosh, etc.), cut into thin wedges
	Lemon juice

In a saucepan, combine beans, Hunt's Tomato Paste, brown sugar, onion and mustard; heat through. Meanwhile, cut bread into five slices; place one slice in each of 5 individual (10-ounce) baking dishes. Cut frankfurters in half crosswise, then in halves lengthwise; stand up, cut side in, around edge of baking dishes. Spoon baked beans in center. Dip apple slices in lemon juice; arrange over beans. Bake at 350°F 20 minutes or until thoroughly heated. Makes 5 servings.

Moussaka Casserole

Easy version of a favorite Greek dish

450 g	1 lb. ground lamb or pork
125 ml	½ cup chopped onion
60 ml	4 Tablesp. pure vegetable oil
	1 eggplant
5 ml	1 teasp. salt
1 ml	¼ teasp. <u>each</u>: nutmeg and pepper
170 g	1 (6-oz.) can Hunt's Tomato Paste
125 ml	½ cup water
110 g	1 (4-oz.) can mushroom stems and pieces, undrained
15 ml	1 Tablesp. butter
125 ml	½ cup soft bread crumbs
85 ml	⅓ cup grated Parmesan cheese
30 ml	2 Tablesp. parsley flakes

In a 10-inch skillet, sauté lamb and onion in *2 tablespoons* oil until onion is soft. Peel eggplant and cut into ½-inch cubes. Add to skillet with *2 tablespoons more* oil; toss to mix. Cook, stirring occasionally, 5 to 10 minutes until eggplant is tender. Add salt, nutmeg and pepper. In a 1½-quart casserole, combine Hunt's Tomato Paste, water and mushrooms. Add eggplant mixture; mix thoroughly. In a small skillet, melt butter. Add bread crumbs, Parmesan and parsley; toss to mix. Sprinkle over casserole. Bake, uncovered, at 400°F 15 to 20 minutes. Makes 6 servings.

Beef Burgundy Bake

Serve-one, save-one casseroles

1350 g	3	lbs. lean stewing beef, cut in 1-inch cubes
180 ml	¾	cup flour
10 ml	2	teasp. salt
125 ml	½	cup pure vegetable oil
	2	cloves garlic, crushed
170 g	1	(6-oz.) can Hunt's Tomato Paste
310 ml	1¼	cups Burgundy or dry red wine
750 ml	3	cups water
5 ml	1	teasp. thyme
	2	bay leaves
220 g	2	(4-oz.) cans mushroom stems and pieces, undrained
225 g	1	(8-oz.) pkg. egg noodle bows, cooked and drained
750 ml	3	cups shredded Cheddar cheese

Coat meat with flour and salt. In large Dutch oven, brown meat, ⅓ at a time, in oil. Return all meat to pan. Add garlic, Hunt's Tomato Paste, wine, water, thyme and bay leaves. Cover; simmer 1½ hours or until meat is tender, stirring occasionally; remove bay leaves. Stir in mushrooms and noodles; pour into 2 (12 x 8 x 2-inch) baking dishes. Bake at 350°F 35 minutes. Border *each* casserole with *half* of cheese. Bake 5 minutes longer. (*OR*: cool, wrap and freeze casserole(s) *before baking*. To serve, thaw at room temperature several hours; cover with foil; bake at 350°F 1 hour. Uncover. Border each with shredded cheese; bake *15* minutes longer.)

Beef Burgundy Bake
Green Beans Amandine
Tossed Green Salad
Sourdough Rolls   Butter
Coffee, Tea or Wine
Sherbet Cups
Assorted Cookies

Each casserole makes 6 servings.

Toreador Pie

Ground beef makes the crust

200 g	1	pkg. (about 7-oz.) Spanish rice-vermicelli mix
30 ml	2	Tablesp. butter or margarine
625 ml	2½	cups hot water
170 g	1	(6-oz.) can Hunt's Tomato Paste
675 g	1½	lbs. lean ground beef
125 ml	½	cup fine dry bread crumbs
5 ml	1	teasp. chili powder
5 ml	1	teasp. salt
.5 ml	⅛	teasp. pepper
	4	slices process American cheese
64 g	1	(2¼-oz.) can sliced ripe olives, drained

In a 10-inch skillet, sauté rice mix in butter until golden, stirring frequently. Slowly stir in hot water, ½ cup Hunt's Tomato Paste and contents of seasoning packet. Cover; simmer 15 minutes or until liquid is almost absorbed. Meanwhile, combine ground beef, bread crumbs, chili powder, salt, pepper and *remaining* Hunt's Tomato Paste in a bowl. Pat firmly over bottom and sides of 9-inch pie pan; build up top edge. Bake at 400°F 15 minutes; drain fat. Dice *half* the cheese slices; fold diced cheese and olives into rice. Spoon into meat shell. Cut *remaining* cheese into strips. Arrange in design over top. Bake 5 minutes longer or until cheese melts. Makes 6 servings.

Breast of Chicken Madras

Luscious spiced fruit sauce

	3	chicken breasts, split
		Salt and pepper
60 ml	¼	cup pure vegetable oil
820 g	1	(1-lb. 13-oz.) can yams, drained
125 ml	½	cup applesauce
60 ml	¼	cup orange juice
45 ml	3	Tablesp. Hunt's Tomato Paste
3 ml	½	teasp. rosemary
1 ml	¼	teasp. cinnamon
5 ml	⅛	teasp. garlic powder

If desired, bone chicken breasts; sprinkle with salt and pepper. In large skillet, quickly brown in hot oil; arrange skin side up with yams in a 2½-quart baking dish. Meanwhile, combine applesauce, orange juice, Hunt's Tomato Paste, rosemary, cinnamon and garlic powder. Spoon over chicken and yams. Bake at 375°F 30 to 35 minutes. Makes 6 servings.

Opposite: Toreador

Southwestern Corned Beef Bake

A shortcut to dinner with pantry-shelf foods

240 g	1	(8½-oz.) pkg. corn muffin mix
450 g	1	(16-oz.) can whole kernel corn, drained
340 g	1	(12-oz.) can corned beef
170 g	1	(6-oz.) can Hunt's Tomato Paste
180 ml	¾	cup water
125 ml	½	cup finely chopped green pepper
125 ml	½	cup chopped onion
15 ml	1	Tablesp. Worcestershire
5 ml	1	teasp. chili powder
5 ml	1	teasp. salt
1 ml	¼	teasp. pepper
	2	slices process American cheese, cut in quarters diagonally

Prepare corn muffin mix according to package directions. Spread batter in bottom of greased 10 x 6 x 2-inch baking dish. Top with corn. Crumble corned beef into bowl and combine with Hunt's Tomato Paste, water, green pepper, onion, Worcestershire, chili powder, salt and pepper; spoon over corn. Top with cheese triangles. Bake at 375°F 25 to 30 minutes. Makes 6 servings.

Eggplant Parmigiana

A little meat adds a lot of flavor

	1	large eggplant
5 ml	1	teasp. salt
125 ml	½	cup pure vegetable oil
170 g	1	(6-oz.) can Hunt's Tomato Paste
250 ml	1	cup water
	1	clove garlic, crushed
5 ml	1	teasp. oregano
1 ml	¼	teasp. pepper
	6	slices salami or ham
	6	slices mozzarella cheese
180 ml	¾	cup grated Parmesan cheese

Peel eggplant; slice ½ inch thick. Sprinkle with salt; brown on both sides in oil. Combine Hunt's Tomato Paste, water, garlic, oregano and pepper in a small bowl. Arrange *half* the eggplant slices in greased 8 x 12 x 2-inch baking dish; cover with *half* the tomato paste mixture, *half* the salami, *half* the mozzarella and *half* the Parmesan. Repeat layers using remaining ingredients. Bake at 350°F 35 to 40 minutes. Makes 6 servings.

Pronto Spanish Rice

Extra quick and easy

450 g	1	lb. frankfurters, thinly sliced
30 ml	2	Tablesp. chopped green pepper
625 ml	2½	cups water
500 ml	2	cups quick-cooking rice
170 g	1	(6-oz.) can Hunt's Tomato Paste
30 ml	2	Tablesp. instant minced onion
10 ml	2	teasp. brown sugar, packed
5 ml	1	teasp. salt
3 ml	½	teasp. chili powder
125 ml	½	cup diced process American cheese

In a large skillet, cook frankfurters and green pepper, stirring, until green pepper is tender. Add remaining ingredients *except* cheese. Bring to boil; stir. Cover; reduce heat and simmer 5 minutes, stirring occasionally. Remove from heat; stir in cheese; cover; let stand 5 minutes before serving. Makes 4 to 6 servings.

Turkey Enchiladas

Low-cost, low-fat turkey with a Mexican flavor

675 g	1½	lbs. ground turkey
500 ml	2	cups shredded jack or mozzarella cheese
64 g	1	(2¼-oz.) can sliced ripe olives, drained
375 ml	1½	cups cottage cheese
	1	dozen corn tortillas
		Pure vegetable oil
110 g	1	(4-oz.) can diced green chilies
	1	large onion, chopped
	1	clove garlic, minced
170 g	1	(6-oz.) can Hunt's Tomato Paste
250 ml	1	cup water
5 ml	1	teasp. oregano
5 ml	1	teasp. salt

In a large skillet, brown turkey; remove from heat. Mix in 1½ *cups* shredded cheese, olives and cottage cheese; set aside. Fry tortillas in oil just until limp. Fill each tortilla with about ⅓ *cup* turkey mixture; roll up and place, seam side down, in 9 x 13 x 2-inch baking dish in single layer. Sauté chilies, onion and garlic in *2 tablespoons oil.* Add Hunt's Tomato Paste, water, oregano and salt; mix well. Simmer 5 minutes. Pour over enchiladas. Sprinkle with *remaining* shredded cheese. Bake at 350°F 25 minutes. Makes 6 servings.

Homespun Sausage Bake

Two Southern favorites team up

450 g	1	lb. bulk pork sausage
250 ml	1	cup chopped onion
250 ml	1	cup sliced celery
170 g	1	(6-oz.) can Hunt's Tomato Paste
250 ml	1	cup water
5 ml	1	teasp. Italian herb seasoning
1 ml	¼	teasp. salt
850 g	1	(1-lb. 14-oz.) can yellow hominy, drained
500 ml	2	cups shredded jack or mozzarella cheese

Brown sausage, onion and celery in skillet; drain fat. Add Hunt's Tomato Paste, water and seasonings; simmer 5 minutes. In 2-quart casserole, layer *half* the hominy, *half* the sausage mixture and *half* the cheese. Repeat layers. Bake at 350°F 25 minutes. Makes 4 to 6 servings.

Pastitsio

Macaroni and cheese, Greek style

675 g	1½	lbs. ground beef
	2	medium onions, chopped
340 g	2	(6-oz.) cans Hunt's Tomato Paste
375 ml	1½	cups water
10 ml	2	teasp. salt
3 ml	½	teasp. pepper
1 ml	¼	teasp. each: cinnamon and nutmeg
205 g	1	(7¼-oz.) pkg. macaroni and cheese dinner
500 ml	2	cups milk
	3	eggs, slightly beaten
125 ml	½	cup grated Parmesan cheese
	4	slices process American cheese, cut in half diagonally

Brown beef and onions in skillet; drain fat. Stir in Hunt's Tomato Paste, water, salt, pepper, cinnamon and nutmeg. Cover and simmer 10 minutes. Meanwhile, cook macaroni according to package directions; drain. Mix contents of cheese sauce packet with milk in saucepan; cook over low heat, stirring until smooth. Add eggs; continue cooking and stirring until sauce is slightly thickened and creamy. Place *half* of cooked macaroni in greased 9 x 13 x 2-inch baking dish; cover with meat mixture. Sprinkle with Parmesan, then *remaining* macaroni. Pour cheese sauce over top. Bake at 325°F 40 minutes or until topping is set. Arrange cheese triangles, overlapping, on top; bake about 2 minutes longer. Makes 8 servings.

posite: Homespun Sausage Bake

Deviled Pork Chop Dinner

The flavors blend to perfection

	6 pork chops, ¾ inch thick
60 ml	¼ cup pure vegetable oil
170 g	1 (6-oz.) can Hunt's Tomato Paste
500 ml	2 cups water
30 ml	2 Tablesp. brown sugar, packed
15 ml	1 Tablesp. lemon juice
	2 chicken bouillon cubes
10 ml	2 teasp. prepared mustard
5 ml	1 teasp. seasoned salt
5 ml	⅛ teasp. pepper
	1 small head cabbage
410 g	1 (14½-oz.) can whole new potatoes, drained
3 ml	½ teasp. caraway seeds

Brown pork chops in oil in 12-inch skillet; drain fat. Combine *next 8* ingredients in a bowl; mix well. Pour all *except ½ cup* of mixture over chops. Cover; simmer 20 minutes. Meanwhile, cut cabbage into small wedges. Cover with boiling water in a bowl; let stand 5 minutes; drain thoroughly. Turn chops; place cabbage wedges and potatoes in sauce between chops. Pour *reserved* sauce over all; sprinkle with caraway seeds. Cover; simmer 25 to 30 minutes longer. Makes 6 servings.

Turkey Tetrazzini

Everyone will sing its praises!

375 ml	1½ cups 1-inch pieces uncooked spaghetti
110 g	1 (4-oz.) can sliced mushrooms, drained
250 ml	1 cup thinly sliced celery
60 ml	¼ cup pure vegetable oil
60 ml	¼ cup flour
170 g	1 (6-oz.) can Hunt's Tomato Paste
250 ml	1 cup turkey or chicken broth
250 ml	1 cup light cream or milk
500 ml	2 cups cubed cooked turkey
5 ml	1 teasp. salt
	Dash pepper
180 ml	¾ cup grated Parmesan cheese

Cook spaghetti according to package directions. Drain; set aside. In a large skillet, cook mushrooms and celery in oil until tender. Add flour; stir until smooth. Mix in Hunt's Tomato Paste, broth and cream, stirring constantly until smooth and thickened. Blend in spaghetti, turkey and seasonings; heat through. Pour into greased 2-quart shallow baking dish. Sprinkle with Parmesan. Place under broiler until golden. Makes 6 to 8 servings.

Chicken and Asparagus Bake

Asparagus-cheese topping makes this unusual, delectable

	3 large whole chicken breasts, split, boned and skinned
	Salt and pepper
30 ml	2 Tablesp. butter
170 g	1 (6-oz.) can Hunt's Tomato Paste
	Water
250 ml	1 cup regular rice
64 g	1 (2¼-oz.) can sliced ripe olives, drained
284 g	1 (10-oz.) pkg. frozen cut asparagus, cooked and drained
250 ml	1 cup ricotta or cottage cheese
	1 egg
1 ml	¼ teasp. marjoram, crumbled
1 ml	¼ teasp. nutmeg
60 ml	¼ cup grated Parmesan cheese

Sprinkle chicken with salt and pepper; brown in butter in skillet. Combine Hunt's Tomato Paste and ¾ *cup water* in a small bowl. In a lightly oiled 9 x 13 x 2-inch baking dish, combine *1 cup* tomato paste mixture with rice, olives, *1 teaspoon* salt and *2 cups* boiling water; arrange chicken over all. Cover dish with foil. Bake at 350°F 35 to 40 minutes. In a bowl, combine asparagus, ricotta cheese, egg, marjoram, nutmeg and ½ *teaspoon* salt. Remove foil from baking dish; drop spoonfuls of asparagus mixture around outer edges and pour *remaining* tomato paste mixture over center. Sprinkle with Parmesan. Bake, uncovered, 10 minutes longer. Makes 6 servings.

Beef 'n Barley Casserole

Hearty whole-meal dish

675 g	1½ lbs. lean ground beef
250 ml	1 cup chopped onion
250 ml	1 cup chopped green pepper
250 ml	1 cup pearl barley, uncooked
450 g	1 (16-oz.) can cut green beans, undrained
410 g	1 (14½-oz.) can Hunt's Whole Tomatoes, undrained
170 g	1 (6-oz.) can Hunt's Tomato Paste
180 ml	¾ cup water
8 ml	1½ teasp. seasoned salt

In a large skillet, brown ground beef, onion and green pepper. Add remaining ingredients; blend well. Pour into greased 2½-quart casserole. Bake, tightly covered, at 350°F 1½ hours. Stir twice during baking. Makes 6 to 8 servings.

Reach for Hunt's Tomato Paste

When Meat Is on the Menu . . .

Turn out delectable main dishes, made special by the great taste of tomato, that the whole family—guests, too—will love. These delicious, varied ways with meat have their origins here at home and around the world. They are all easy to make, use ingredients you have at hand or can come by readily—including tomato paste, the one ingredient common to all that makes them all so good.

Opposite: Far Eastern Beef and Noodles (see page

Far Eastern Beef and Noodles

(Illustrated page 45)

A conversation piece for looks and taste

450 g	1	lb. beef top round
20 ml	4	teasp. soy sauce
15 ml	1	Tablesp. cornstarch
142 g	1	(about 5-oz.) pkg. instant Oriental noodles
750 ml	3	cups sliced Chinese cabbage
60 ml	¼	cup pure vegetable oil
		Ginger Sauce (recipe follows)
	2	green onions, chopped

Cut beef in half lengthwise. Cut across grain in ¼-inch-thick slices. Combine in a bowl with soy sauce and cornstarch; set aside. Cook noodles according to package directions. Lift noodles from water with slotted spoon to hot serving platter. *Return water to boiling.* Add cabbage and cook 1 minute; drain. Spoon over noodles. Meanwhile, heat oil in skillet; add beef mixture and stir-fry until just cooked. Spoon over cabbage. Pour Ginger Sauce over all. Garnish with onion. Makes 4 servings.

Ginger Sauce

170 g	1	(6-oz.) can Hunt's Tomato Paste
250 ml	1	cup water
15 ml	1	Tablesp. soy sauce
15 ml	1	Tablesp. brown sugar
5 ml	1	teasp. salt
5 ml	1	teasp. ground ginger

Combine all ingredients in saucepan. Simmer 5 minutes, stirring occasionally, until thickened. Makes 1½ cups sauce.

Beef Stroganoff

Popular dish for family or company

900 g	2	lbs. boneless chuck steak, cut into ¼-inch strips
45 ml	3	Tablesp. pure vegetable oil
	1	large onion, chopped
110 g	1	(4-oz.) can sliced mushrooms, drained
170 g	1	(6-oz.) can Hunt's Tomato Paste
310 ml	1¼	cups water
5 ml	1	teasp. salt
15 ml	1	Tablesp. Worcestershire
125 ml	½	cup sour cream

In a large skillet, brown meat in hot oil. Remove meat. Sauté onion and mushrooms in skillet drippings until golden brown. Stir in remaining ingredients, *except* sour cream. Return meat to pan. Cover; simmer, stirring occasionally, about 30 minutes or until meat is tender. Remove from heat. Gradually stir in sour cream; blend well. Serve over rice or noodles, as desired. Makes 6 servings.

Tempura — California Style

Beef and vegetables in a delicate batter

675 g	1	beef flank steak (about 1½ lbs.)
	1	bunch green onions
	12	mushrooms
	8	sprigs parsley
	2	medium zucchini
250 ml	1	cup ice water
250 ml	1	cup flour
8 ml	1½	teasp. sugar
5 ml	1	teasp. soy sauce
3 ml	½	teasp. salt
1 ml	¼	teasp. baking soda
	1	egg yolk
		Pure vegetable oil
		Sweet and Sour Sauce (recipe follows)

Trim fat from flank steak; cut across grain into thin diagonal slices about 3 inches long. Cut green onions and tops into 2-inch pieces. Wash mushrooms. Break parsley into sprigs. Quarter zucchini lengthwise and cut into 2-inch sticks. Combine ice water, flour, seasonings, soda and egg yolk in a bowl; beat until smooth. Fill deep fryer or heavy kettle to ⅓ its depth with oil. Heat slowly to 375°F. Dip meat and vegetables into batter a few at a time. Lower carefully into preheated oil. Cook a few at a time, turning occasionally, until golden brown. Serve with Sweet and Sour Sauce. Makes 6 servings.

Tempura—California Style
Hot Steamed Rice
Oriental Cucumber Salad
Tea
Chilled Mandarin Oranges
Almond Cookies

Sweet and Sour Sauce

170 g	1	(6-oz.) can Hunt's Tomato Paste
250 ml	1	cup pineapple juice
125 ml	½	cup water
60 ml	¼	cup brown sugar, packed
30 ml	2	Tablesp. cornstarch
30 ml	2	Tablesp. vinegar
3 ml	½	teasp. salt
3 ml	½	teasp. ground ginger

Combine all ingredients in saucepan. Bring to boil, stirring constantly; lower heat and stir until mixture thickens. Makes about 2 cups.

48 **Braised Oxtails with Vegetables**

A marvelous blend of flavors

1800 g	4	lbs. sliced oxtails
		Salt and pepper
	1	medium onion
450 g	1	lb. carrots
45 ml	3	Tablesp. pure vegetable oil
60 ml	¼	cup flour
3 ml	½	teasp. thyme
170 g	1	(6-oz.) can Hunt's Tomato Paste
750 ml	3	cups water
125 ml	½	cup dry red wine (optional)
	3	beef bouillon cubes
	4	turnips

Trim excess fat from oxtails; sprinkle with salt and pepper. Arrange in greased 9 × 13 × 2-inch baking pan. Bake at 450°F 30 minutes. Chop onion and ½ *cup* carrots. Sauté in a skillet in oil, stirring, until onion is transparent. Sprinkle with flour, thyme and ½ *teaspoon* salt. Toss to mix thoroughly. Remove oxtails from oven; turn; cover with sautéed vegetables. Bake at 450°F 15 minutes longer. Meanwhile, combine Hunt's Tomato Paste, water, wine and bouillon cubes in skillet. Bring to boil. Pour over oxtails and vegetables. Cover tightly. *Lower oven temperature to 325°F;* bake 3 hours. Slice *remaining* carrots; peel and quarter turnips. Add to oxtails, pressing them into the liquid. Cover and bake 30 to 40 minutes longer. Makes 4 to 6 servings.

Swiss Steak, Sunday Style

Family favorite any day of the week

900 g	2	lbs. round steak, ½ inch thick
45 ml	3	Tablesp. flour
5 ml	1	teasp. salt
1 ml	¼	teasp. pepper
45 ml	3	Tablesp. pure vegetable oil
	1	onion, sliced
170 g	1	(6-oz.) can Hunt's Tomato Paste
500 ml	2	cups water
5 ml	1	teasp. sugar
284 g	1	(10-oz.) pkg. frozen peas and carrots.

Cut steak into serving pieces; pound in mixture of flour, salt and pepper. In large skillet, brown steak on both sides in hot oil; remove steak. Brown onion in drippings. Blend in Hunt's Tomato Paste, water and sugar, stirring until smooth. Return steak to skillet; cover tightly. Lower heat; simmer 1 to 1½ hours or until steak is tender. Add peas and carrots last 10 minutes. Makes 6 to 8 servings.

Beef Braciola

Tender rolls of beef, salami, mozzarella in unsurpassed sauce

900 g	2	lbs. top round steak
		Garlic salt
	16	slices Italian dry salami
375 ml	1½	cups shredded mozzarella
45 ml	3	Tablesp. pure vegetable oil
170 g	1	(6-oz.) can Hunt's Tomato Paste
250 ml	1	cup water
250 ml	1	cup canned beef broth
60 ml	¼	cup Chablis or dry white wine
	1	bay leaf
5 ml	1	teasp. sugar
3 ml	½	teasp. oregano
1 ml	¼	teasp. thyme
250 ml	1	cup thinly sliced zucchini
284 g	1	(10-oz.) pkg. fettucine or egg noodles, cooked and drained

Trim fat from beef; pound with mallet to ⅛-inch thickness. Sprinkle lightly with garlic salt. Cut into 8 pieces. Top with salami and mozzarella. Roll up and secure with toothpicks. Brown in oil in large skillet; drain fat. In a bowl, combine *remaining* ingredients *except* zucchini and fettucine; mix well. Pour over meat rolls. Cover; simmer 30 minutes. Add zucchini. Cover; simmer 30 minutes longer. Arrange meat rolls and zucchini on bed of fettucine. Thicken skillet juices and serve with meat rolls. Makes 4 to 6 servings.

Old-Time BBQ Beef

Long, slow cooking is the flavor secret

1350 g	3	lbs. fresh beef brisket
3 ml	½	teasp. garlic salt
3 ml	½	teasp. celery salt
3 ml	½	teasp. onion powder or juice
60 ml	¼	cup liquid smoke
170 g	1	(6-oz.) can Hunt's Tomato Paste
250 ml	1	cup water
250 ml	1	cup prepared barbecue sauce
60 ml	¼	cup brown sugar, packed
3 ml	½	teasp. salt

Rub both sides of beef with garlic salt, celery salt, and onion powder. Place in shallow glass baking dish. Spread liquid smoke on both sides of meat. Cover tightly with foil; refrigerate overnight. Combine remaining ingredients in slow cooker; add beef; cover. Cook 8 to 10 hours on *low* setting or 5 to 6 hours on *medium* setting. Serve thinly sliced; top with sauce. Makes 6 servings.

Farmer's Pork Chops

Satisfying all-in-one skillet supper

	6	lean pork chops, cut 1 inch thick
60 ml	¼	cup flour
10 ml	2	teasp. salt
10 ml	2	teasp. caraway seeds
45 ml	3	Tablesp. pure vegetable oil
	1	large knockwurst, thinly sliced
250 ml	1	cup chopped celery
	1	onion, chopped
	2	sweet pickles, diced
1 ml	¼	teasp. pepper
170 g	1	(6-oz.) can Hunt's Tomato Paste
298 g	1	(10½-oz.) can beef broth
250 ml	1	cup water
	2	large potatoes, peeled and sliced

Trim fat from chops; coat with mixture of flour, *1 teaspoon* salt and *1 teaspoon* caraway seeds. In large skillet, brown chops on both sides in oil; remove chops and drain fat. To skillet add knockwurst, celery, onion and pickles; sprinkle with pepper and *remaining* salt and caraway seeds. Return chops to skillet. In a bowl, combine Hunt's Tomato Paste, beef broth and water. Arrange potatoes over meat; pour tomato paste mixture over all. Simmer, covered, 35 to 45 minutes. Makes 6 servings.

Barbecued Ribs

Best-ever ribs

2250 g	4	to 5 lbs. spareribs, cut into serving-size pieces
		Salt and pepper
		Garlic salt
170 g	1	(6-oz.) can Hunt's Tomato Paste
125 ml	½	cup water
60 ml	¼	cup vinegar
30 ml	2	Tablesp. molasses
15 ml	1	Tablesp. prepared mustard
15 ml	1	Tablesp. instant minced onion
15 ml	1	Tablesp. Worcestershire
5 ml	1	teasp. salt
.5 ml	⅛	teasp. liquid smoke flavoring

Sprinkle ribs with salt, pepper and garlic salt. Place in shallow roasting pan. Bake at 450°F 30 minutes; pour off fat. Meanwhile, combine remaining ingredients in a small bowl. *Reduce oven to 350°F.* Brush ribs with sauce; continue baking about 1 hour, basting occasionally with sauce. Turn once during baking. Makes 5 to 6 servings.

posite: Farmer's Pork Chops

Veal Roll-Ups Italiano

Meltingly tender with ham-and-cheese filling

	4	veal cutlets, about ¼ inch thick
		Salt and pepper
	4	thin slices mozzarella or Swiss cheese
	4	thin slices cooked ham
60 ml	¼	cup pure vegetable oil
170 g	1	(6-oz.) can Hunt's Tomato Paste
310 ml	1¼	cups water
	1	onion, chopped
110 g	1	(4-oz.) can whole mushrooms, drained
	1	bay leaf
	1	clove garlic, minced
60 ml	¼	cup minced parsley
60 ml	¼	cup Marsala or dry red wine

Pound meat with mallet or edge of saucer until about ⅛ inch thick. Sprinkle lightly with salt and pepper. Place 1 slice cheese and 1 slice ham on each veal slice. Starting at narrow end, tightly roll each meat slice jelly-roll fashion; secure with toothpicks. In skillet, brown rolls in oil; drain fat. Combine Hunt's Tomato Paste and water; pour over rolls. Add onion, mushrooms, bay leaf, garlic and parsley. Cover; simmer 20 minutes. Add wine; simmer, covered, 25 to 30 minutes longer or until meat is tender. Makes 4 servings.

Pork Chops and Rice Indienne

Wild-rice mixture dresses up chops

	4	center-cut pork chops, ½ inch thick
30 ml	2	Tablesp. pure vegetable oil
		Salt and pepper
170 g	1	(6-oz.) pkg. long grain and wild rice with herbs and seasonings
170 g	1	(6-oz.) can Hunt's Tomato Paste
500 ml	2	cups water
	2	chicken bouillon cubes
60 ml	¼	cup golden raisins
	4	thin slices onion
	4	thin rings of green pepper
60 ml	¼	cup chopped salted peanuts

In a 10-inch skillet, brown pork chops in oil on each side; sprinkle with salt and pepper. Remove. Add rice and seasoning packet, Hunt's Tomato Paste, water, bouillon cubes and raisins. Blend well. Arrange pork chops on rice; top with onion slices and green pepper rings. Cover; simmer 45 minutes. Sprinkle peanuts over top before serving. Makes 4 servings.

Sunday Sauerbraten

Cooks while you're away

1800 g	4	lb. round or O-bone beef roast
170 g	1	(6-oz.) can Hunt's Tomato Paste
250 ml	1	cup water
125 ml	½	cup vinegar
28 g	1	env. (about 1-oz.) all-purpose meat marinade mix
	1	onion, sliced
	¼	teasp. coarsely ground pepper
	2	bay leaves
.5 ml	⅛	teasp. allspice
	12	gingersnaps, crushed
10 ml	2	teasp. sugar
	1	small head red cabbage

Place roast in heavy kettle or Dutch oven; pierce surface with meat fork. In a bowl, combine Hunt's Tomato Paste with water, vinegar and marinade mix. Pour over roast; let stand 15 minutes, turning occasionally. Add onion and spices. Bring to boil; cover; simmer gently 2½ to 3 hours. Remove bay leaves. Stir in gingersnaps and sugar. Cut cabbage into 8 wedges; add to kettle. Cover; simmer about 20 to 25 minutes longer. Makes 6 to 8 servings.

Hungarian Goulash

Rich sauce, robust flavor you will love

	3	onions, sliced
85 ml	⅓	cup pure vegetable oil
30 ml	2	Tablesp. paprika
10 ml	2	teasp. salt
1 ml	¼	teasp. pepper
1350 g	3	lbs. boneless pork shoulder, cut in 1½-inch cubes
170 g	1	(6-oz.) can Hunt's Tomato Paste
375 ml	1½	cups water
	1	clove garlic, minced
125 ml	½	cup sour cream (optional)

In a Dutch oven, cook onions in oil until tender, stirring frequently; remove and reserve. Combine paprika, *1 teaspoon* salt and the pepper; coat meat with mixture. Brown meat in drippings; drain fat. Return onions to pan. Stir in Hunt's Tomato Paste, water, garlic and *remaining* salt. Simmer, stirring occasionally, for 1½ to 2 hours or until meat is tender. (If too thick, stir in a bit more water.) Garnish servings with sour cream, if desired. Makes 6 to 8 servings.

Reach for Hunt's Tomato Paste

When Poultry Is on the Menu . . .

Chicken is a favorite with almost everyone, but the old ways with chicken can become the we're-tired-of-it ways if they appear on your table too often. And certainly there's a limit to the number of roast turkeys you can serve. Browse here for some exciting new poultry dishes and great ways with leftovers, too. You and your family will become poultry lovers all over again.

Opposite: Cornish Hens à l'Orange (see page 56)

Cornish Hens à l'Orange (Illustrated page 55)

Serve this for a special occasion

170 g	1	(6-oz.) can Hunt's Tomato Paste
375 ml	1½	cups chicken broth
125 ml	½	cup diced celery
30 ml	2	Tablesp. sliced green onion
		Brown sugar
3 ml	½	teasp. salt
375 ml	1½	cups quick-cooking rice
3 ml	½	teasp. grated orange rind
	4	Cornish game hens
60 ml	¼	cup orange juice
60 ml	¼	cup pure vegetable oil

In a saucepan, mix Hunt's Tomato Paste and broth until smooth. *Reserve ¾ cup for basting sauce.* Add celery, green onion, *2 tablespoons* brown sugar and salt to remaining mixture in saucepan; bring to boil. Stir in quick-cooking rice and orange rind. Cover; let stand 5 minutes or until moisture is absorbed. Wash Cornish hens, pat dry. Stuff with rice mixture; place breast side up on a greased jelly roll pan. To make basting sauce, combine *reserved* tomato paste mixture, orange juice, oil and *2 tablespoons* brown sugar. Brush Cornish hens with basting sauce. Bake at 400°F 1 hour or until tender, basting often. If Cornish hens begin to brown too much, cover lightly with foil. Makes 4 to 6 servings.

Glazed Turkey, Winter Style

Turkey with a new look and taste

2700 g	1	turkey half (5 to 6 lbs.)
		Heavy-duty aluminum foil
		Salt and pepper
45 ml	3	Tablesp. pure vegetable oil
170 g	1	(6-oz.) can Hunt's Tomato Paste
180 ml	¾	cup carbonated lemon-lime beverage
125 ml	½	cup water
85 ml	⅓	cup brown sugar, packed

Rinse turkey with cold water; pat dry. Lay turkey skin side up on large sheet of foil; sprinkle with salt and pepper; brush with oil. Double-fold sides of foil over top of turkey; shape open ends of foil up to retain juices. Place in shallow roasting pan. Bake at 400°F about 2½ hours, basting every half hour with drippings. Meanwhile, combine *remaining* ingredients in saucepan; simmer 5 minutes. Fold foil back; bake 1 hour longer, basting every 20 minutes with sauce. Serve remaining sauce with turkey. Makes 6 to 8 servings.

Turkey Paprika

Marvelous Hungarian flavor and flair

	1 onion, sliced and separated into rings
	1 clove garlic, crushed
30 ml	2 Tablesp. butter or margarine
500 ml	2 cups diced cooked turkey
500 ml	2 cups turkey or chicken broth
170 g	1 (6-oz.) can Hunt's Tomato Paste
30 ml	2 Tablesp. paprika
	Hot buttered noodles
	Poppy or caraway seeds
250 ml	1 cup sour cream

In a skillet, cook onion and garlic in butter until onion is limp. Add turkey, broth, Hunt's Tomato Paste and paprika; mix well. Simmer 15 minutes. Serve on a bed of hot buttered noodles tossed with either poppy or caraway seeds. Just before serving, top with spoonfuls of sour cream. Makes 6 servings.

Country Kitchen Chicken

Summer squash adds homey goodness

1350 g	3 lbs. frying chicken pieces
60 ml	¼ cup pure vegetable oil
	1 large onion, thinly sliced
170 g	1 (6-oz.) can Hunt's Tomato Paste
250 ml	1 cup chicken broth
	1 bay leaf
5 ml	1 teasp. salt
3 ml	½ teasp. pepper
	4 medium summer squash (zucchini, crookneck, etc.), cut in ½-inch pieces
110 g	4 ozs. wide noodles, cooked and drained
	Snipped fresh parsley

In a large heavy skillet, brown chicken in oil; remove chicken. Cook onion in drippings until transparent; drain fat. Return chicken to skillet. In a bowl, combine Hunt's Tomato Paste, broth, bay leaf, salt and pepper. Pour over chicken; simmer, covered, 30 minutes. Add squash; simmer, covered, 20 to 25 minutes longer or until chicken and vegetables are tender. Remove bay leaf. Arrange chicken and vegetables on heated serving platter; pour sauce over all. Border with hot noodles and sprinkle with parsley. Makes 4 to 5 servings.

Turkey Parmigiana

Economical turkey substitutes for veal

450 g	10	to 12 ¼-inch-thick slices of cooked turkey (about 1 lb.)
	1	egg
15 ml	1	Tablesp. water
3 ml	½	teasp. salt
.5 ml	⅛	teasp. pepper
85 ml	⅓	cup grated Parmesan cheese
85 ml	⅓	cup fine dry bread crumbs
60 ml	¼	cup finely chopped onion
30 ml	2	Tablesp. pure vegetable oil
170 g	1	(6-oz.) can Hunt's Tomato Paste
180 ml	¾	cup water
125 ml	½	cup dry white wine or turkey broth
4 ml	¾	teasp. oregano
170 g	6	ozs. sliced mozzarella or Swiss cheese

Dip turkey in egg beaten with water, salt and pepper. Coat with mixture of Parmesan cheese and bread crumbs. Place in well-oiled shallow baking dish. Bake at 400°F 15 minutes. Meanwhile, lightly brown onion in oil in a saucepan. Add Hunt's Tomato Paste, water, wine and oregano; mix well; pour over turkey. Arrange cheese slices over turkey. *Reduce heat to 350°F*; bake 20 minutes longer. Makes 5 to 6 servings.

Chicken Aloha

Try this at your next party

2250 g	4	to 5 lbs. frying chicken pieces
45 ml	3	Tablesp. pure vegetable oil
1120 g	2	(20-oz.) cans pineapple chunks in their own juice
170 g	1	(6-oz.) can Hunt's Tomato Paste
125 ml	½	cup <u>each</u>: cider vinegar, light corn syrup and brown sugar, packed
30 ml	2	Tablesp. cornstarch
5 ml	1	teasp. salt
1 ml	¼	teasp. pepper
		Hot cooked rice

Brush chicken pieces lightly with oil. Bake in 2 (9 × 13 × 2-inch) pans at 375°F 45 minutes; drain fat. Meanwhile, drain pineapple, *reserving 1½ cups pineapple juice*. In a saucepan, thoroughly mix pineapple juice with remaining ingredients *except* rice and pineapple chunks. Simmer, stirring constantly, until mixture is clear and thickened. Arrange pineapple chunks over chicken; pour sauce over all. Bake 30 minutes longer. Serve with hot cooked rice. Makes 8 servings.

Chicken Bengalese

A favorite from India adapted for American tastes

1350 g	1	(2½- to 3-lb.) frying chicken, cut up
125 ml	½	cup flour
		Salt
3 ml	½	teasp. pepper
85 ml	⅓	cup pure vegetable oil
	1	medium onion, thinly sliced
125 ml	½	cup sliced celery
	1	clove garlic, crushed
170 g	1	(6-oz.) can Hunt's Tomato Paste
500 ml	2	cups water
5 ml	1	teasp. curry powder
750 ml	3	cups hot cooked rice
125 ml	½	cup raisins
60 ml	¼	cup chopped salted peanuts

Coat chicken with flour mixed with *1 teaspoon* salt and pepper. In skillet, brown chicken in oil; remove. Add onion, celery and garlic; cook in drippings until transparent; drain fat. Add Hunt's Tomato Paste, water, curry and ½ *teaspoon* salt, stirring until smooth. Return chicken to skillet. Cover; simmer 45 minutes or until tender. Toss rice with raisins. Serve with chicken and sauce. Sprinkle nuts over all. Makes 4 to 6 servings.

Turkey Stew

A new way with leftover turkey

500 ml	2	cups chopped cooked turkey
1250 ml	5	cups water
	1	carrot, finely chopped
170 g	1	(6-oz.) can Hunt's Tomato Paste
440 ml	1	(15½-oz.) can small red beans, drained
15 ml	1	Tablesp. instant minced onion
	2	chicken bouillon cubes
5 ml	1	teasp. salt
1000 ml	4	cups shredded cabbage (½ medium head)

In a Dutch oven or large kettle, combine all ingredients *except* cabbage. Bring to boil and simmer 10 minutes. Add cabbage; simmer 10 minutes longer or until cabbage is tender. Makes 6 servings.

When cooked ... brown rice and long- or short-grain white rice triple in volume. Quick-cooking rice almost doubles.

Rancho Chicken

Southwestern flavors in a handsome casserole

1350 g	1	(2½- to 3-lb.) frying chicken, cut up
125 ml	½	cup flour
5 ml	1	teasp. salt
1 ml	¼	teasp. pepper
60 ml	¼	cup pure vegetable oil
250 ml	1	cup chopped onion
250 ml	1	cup chopped green pepper
450 g	1	(16-oz.) can cream style corn
64 g	1	(2¼-oz.) can sliced ripe olives, drained
170 g	1	(6-oz.) can Hunt's Tomato Paste
250 ml	1	cup water
5 ml	1	teasp. chili powder

Coat chicken with flour mixed with salt and pepper. In large skillet, brown chicken in oil; place chicken in 9 × 13 × 2-inch baking dish. Sauté onion and green pepper in skillet drippings until tender. Arrange onion, green pepper, corn and olives over chicken. In a bowl, thoroughly blend Hunt's Tomato Paste, water and chili powder; pour over chicken. Cover; bake at 350°F 1 hour. Makes 5 to 6 servings.

Chicken Italienne

Tastes as good as it looks

1350 g	3	lbs. frying chicken pieces
45 ml	3	Tablesp. pure vegetable oil
180 ml	¾	cup water
170 g	1	(6-oz.) can Hunt's Tomato Paste
110 g	1	(4-oz.) can button mushrooms, undrained
	1	clove garlic, crushed
250 ml	1	cup chicken broth
85 ml	⅓	cup minced onion
60 ml	¼	cup dry red wine
30 ml	2	Tablesp. minced parsley
5 ml	1	teasp. Italian herb seasoning
3 ml	½	teasp. sugar
225 g	8	ozs. spinach or egg noodles, cooked and drained
30 ml	2	Tablesp. flour

Brown chicken in oil in 12-inch skillet; drain fat. Combine ½ cup water and remaining ingredients except noodles and flour; mix well. Pour over chicken. Cover; simmer 30 minutes. Arrange chicken on noodles on warm platter. Combine remaining water and flour and use to thicken skillet juices. Serve with chicken and noodles. Makes 4 to 6 servings.

Opposite: Rancho Chi

Reach for Hunt's Tomato Paste

When There's Ground Beef– Again! . . .

Ground beef is a fact of life for most families—and fortunately, most families, bless them, love it. Now is the time to take a new look at the familiar standby. Experiment with these variations on the theme, and you'll make yourself and your family happy. Go ahead, buy ground beef again and have fun serving it in one of these inventive dishes.

Opposite: Meat Loaf Under Wraps (see page 6-

Meat Loaf Under Wraps (Illustrated page 63)

Potato "frosting" gives meat loaf new stature

170 g	1	(6-oz.) can Hunt's Tomato Paste
375 ml	1½	cups water
675 g	1½	lbs. lean ground beef
250 ml	1	cup fine cracker crumbs
125 ml	½	cup <u>each</u>: finely chopped onion and green pepper
	2	eggs, separated
3 ml	½	teasp. salt
1 ml	¼	teasp. pepper
750 ml	3	cups hot prepared mashed potatoes
60 ml	¼	cup shredded Cheddar cheese
15 ml	1	Tablesp. butter
30 ml	2	Tablesp. brown sugar, packed
30 ml	2	Tablesp. Worcestershire
30 ml	2	Tablesp. mushroom stems and pieces

Blend together Hunt's Tomato Paste and water in small saucepan; set aside. Combine in a bowl ½ *cup* tomato paste mixture, ground beef, cracker crumbs, onion, green pepper, *egg whites*, salt and pepper; mix well. Shape mixture into a loaf in a shallow baking dish. Bake at 350°F 45 minutes. Meanwhile, in a saucepan, combine hot prepared mashed potatoes, cheese, butter and *egg yolks*. Stir and heat 2 to 5 minutes to melt cheese. Drain fat from meat loaf; frost with potato mixture. Bake 15 to 20 minutes longer. Add brown sugar, Worcestershire and mushrooms to saucepan of remaining tomato paste mixture; heat 3 to 5 minutes. Serve over slices of meat loaf. Makes 6 to 8 servings.

Sloppy Joes

Biggest sandwich favorite since the burger

450 g	1	lb. lean ground beef
	3	slices bacon, cut in 1-inch pieces
	1	onion, chopped
170 g	1	(6-oz.) can Hunt's Tomato Paste
310 ml	1¼	cups water
35 g	1	(1¼-oz.) env. sloppy joe seasoning mix
		Hamburger buns, toasted

In a 10-inch skillet, sauté ground beef, bacon and onion until beef loses its redness; drain fat. Add *remaining* ingredients *except* hamburger buns. Simmer 15 to 20 minutes over low heat. Stir occasionally. Serve between toasted buns. Makes 8 to 10 sandwiches.

Sweet and Sour Meatballs

Scrumptious as appetizer or entrée

900 g	2 lbs. lean ground beef
250 ml	1 cup soft bread crumbs
	1 egg, beaten
10 ml	2 teasp. instant minced onion
5 ml	1 teasp. seasoned salt
3 ml	½ teasp. garlic powder
30 ml	2 Tablesp. cornstarch
45 ml	3 Tablesp. brown sugar, packed
5 ml	1 teasp. salt
125 ml	½ cup each: orange juice and vinegar
170 g	1 (6-oz.) can Hunt's Tomato Paste
500 ml	2 cups water
230 g	1 (8¼-oz.) can sliced pineapple, undrained and quartered
	1 green pepper, cut in 1-inch squares
250 ml	1 cup sliced celery
	1 onion, cut in eighths

In a medium bowl, combine ground beef, bread crumbs, egg, minced onion, salt and garlic powder; form into 40 (1-inch) meatballs. Brown meatballs *half* at a time in a Dutch oven; drain fat. *Remove meatballs and set aside*. In a small bowl, combine cornstarch, brown sugar and salt; stir in orange juice and vinegar until well blended. Add, with Hunt's Tomato Paste and water, to Dutch oven; blend well. Add pineapple, green pepper, celery and onion. Bring to a boil, stirring. Lower heat; simmer, stirring often, until sauce is thickened and transparent. Return meatballs; simmer 10 to 15 minutes longer or until vegetables are crisp-tender. Serve as an appetizer or over hot cooked rice as an entée. Makes (40 meatballs) 8 to 10 servings.

Quick-and-Easy Chili

Fastest chili in the West

450 g	1 lb. lean ground beef
	1 onion, chopped
35 g	1 (1¼-oz.) env. chili seasoning mix
5 ml	1 teasp. salt
340 g	2 (6-oz.) or 1 (12-oz.) can Hunt's Tomato Paste
625 ml	2½ cups water
850 g	2 (15-oz.) cans chili beans, undrained

Sauté ground beef and onion in a Dutch oven; drain fat. Stir in chili seasoning and salt. Add remaining ingredients; mix well. Simmer covered, 20 to 25 minutes. Stir occasionally. Makes 2 quarts.

Tacos

Mexican-style sandwich

450 g	1	lb. lean ground beef
35 g	1	(1¼-oz.) env. taco seasoning mix
5 ml	1	teasp. seasoned salt
170 g	1	(6-oz.) can Hunt's Tomato Paste
180 ml	¾	cup water
		Prepared taco shells
375 ml	1½	cups shredded lettuce
250 ml	1	cup shredded Cheddar cheese
250 ml	1	cup chopped tomatoes

Sauté ground beef in 10-inch skillet until beef loses its redness; drain fat. Stir in taco seasoning, salt, Hunt's Tomato Paste and water. Simmer over medium heat 5 to 10 minutes. Stir occasionally. Fill each taco shell with a layer of ground beef mixture; top with lettuce, cheese and tomatoes. Makes 10 to 12 tacos.

Enchiladas

Hunt's version of a Mexican favorite

To make your own taco shells . . .
In a heavy skillet, heat 1 inch of oil to 375°F. Fold corn tortilla in half; holding edges together with tongs, fry until crisp.

340 g	2	(6-oz.) or 1 (12-oz.) can Hunt's Tomato Paste
1000 ml	1	qt. water
	2	cloves garlic, minced
25 ml	5	teasp. chili powder
10 ml	2	teasp. salt
3 ml	½	teasp. ground cumin
1 ml	¼	teasp. Tabasco
450 g	1	lb. lean ground beef
125 ml	½	cup chopped green onions
500 ml	2	cups shredded Monterey Jack cheese
125 ml	½	cup sliced ripe olives
	1	doz. corn tortillas

In a saucepan, combine Hunt's Tomato Paste, water, garlic, chili powder, salt, cumin and Tabasco; simmer 20 minutes. In skillet, brown ground beef with *half* the onions; drain fat. Stir in 1½ *cups* cheese, *1 cup* tomato paste mixture and *half* the olives. Spoon ¼ *cup* tomato paste mixture in 3-quart shallow baking dish. Soften tortillas one at a time by dipping in and out of *remaining* mixture. Spoon beef mixture down center of each tortilla; roll up, place seam side down in baking dish. Pour *remaining* tomato paste mixture over top. Sprinkle with *remaining* cheese, onions and olives. Bake at 350°F 20 minutes or until hot and bubbly. Makes 6 servings.

Saucy Blue Cheese Burgers

Nippy sauced hamburgers on sourdough slices — makes burgers proud!

170 g	1	(6-oz.) can Hunt's Tomato Paste
250 ml	1	cup water
5 ml	1	teasp. <u>each</u>: salt and sugar
675 g	1½	lbs. lean ground beef
30 ml	2	Tablesp. instant minced onion
15 ml	1	Tablesp. Worcestershire
5 ml	1	teasp. seasoned salt
3 ml	½	teasp. garlic powder
60 ml	¼	cup <u>each:</u> crumbled blue cheese and mayonnaise
		Sliced sourdough bread

Blend together Hunt's Tomato Paste, water, salt and sugar in a bowl. Add ⅓ *cup* to ground beef, onion, Worcestershire, seasoned salt and garlic powder. Mix well; form into 8 patties. Combine blue cheese and mayonnaise; spread *1 tablespoon* on each of *4* patties. Top with *remaining* patties; pinch edges together. Brown patties in skillet on both sides; drain fat. Blend together *remaining* tomato paste mixture and blue cheese mixture. Pour over cooked patties. Simmer 5 to 10 minutes. Serve open-faced on sliced sourdough bread. Makes 4 servings.

Stuffed Cabbage Rolls

A variation on an old favorite

	1	head of cabbage
		Boiling water
170 g	1	(6-oz.) can Hunt's Tomato Paste
298 g	1	(10½-oz.) can beef bouillon
450 g	1	lb. lean ground beef, cooked
250 ml	1	cup cubed Cheddar cheese
30 ml	2	Tablesp. instant minced onion
3 ml	½	teasp. salt
1 ml	¼	teasp. pepper

Core cabbage; place in bowl, cored side up. Pour boiling water over to cover; let stand 3 to 5 minutes or until leaves will separate and fold without breaking. In skillet, blend together Hunt's Tomato Paste and beef bouillon. In small bowl, add ½ *cup* tomato paste mixture to cooked ground beef, cheese, onion, salt and pepper. Place equal portions of meat mixture in center of each cabbage leaf. Fold sides of leaf over meat; roll up and place seam side down in skillet of *remaining* tomato paste mixture. Spoon a little sauce mixture over cabbage rolls. Simmer, covered, over medium heat 25 to 35 minutes. Makes 4 to 6 servings.

Ground Beef Fillets

Ground beef and bacon with a zippy basting sauce

900 g	2 lbs. ground beef
250 ml	1 cup seasoned bread crumbs
30 ml	2 Tablesp. instant minced onion
3 ml	½ teasp. salt
	1 egg
170 g	1 (6-oz.) can Hunt's Tomato Paste
180 ml	¾ cup water
	8 slices bacon
60 ml	¼ cup steak sauce

In a bowl, combine ground beef, bread crumbs, onion, salt and egg. Mix together Hunt's Tomato Paste and water. Add ½ *cup* to meat; *reserve remaining*. Blend well. Shape into 8 patties; wrap each with a slice of bacon and secure with toothpick. Place on rack in jelly roll pan. Broil patties about five minutes on each side. Add steak sauce to *reserved* tomato paste mixture. Brush lightly on each side; cook 1 to 2 minutes longer. Makes 8 servings.

Zucchini Boats

Savory all-in-one meat-and-vegetable dish

	8 medium zucchini, halved lengthwise
450 g	1 lb. ground beef
170 ml	⅔ cup chopped green pepper
170 ml	⅔ cup chopped onion
170 g	1 (6 oz.) can Hunt's Tomato Paste
250 ml	1 cup water
5 ml	1 teasp. <u>each</u>: oregano and salt
3 ml	½ teasp. basil
1 ml	¼ teasp. garlic powder
	Dash pepper
	Parmesan cheese

Parboil zucchini halves 10 to 15 minutes or until tender; drain well. Cool 5 to 10 minutes. Meanwhile, in a skillet, brown beef, green pepper and onion; drain fat. Stir in Hunt's Tomato Paste, water and seasonings. Reduce heat, simmer 10 minutes, stirring occasionally. Hollow out zucchini to form shells, adding pulp to meat mixture. Arrange zucchini shells in 9 × 13 × 2-inch baking dish. Fill center of each with equal portion of meat mixture. Top with Parmesan cheese. Place under broiler 3 to 5 minutes to brown and melt cheese. Makes 6 to 8 servings.

Opposite: Ground Beef Fil

Chili Beef Bundles

Spicy beef filling in a tender crust

450 g	1	lb. lean ground beef
125 ml	½	cup chopped onion
170 g	1	(6-oz.) can Hunt's Tomato Paste
35 g	1	(1¼-oz.) env. chili seasoning mix
310 ml	1¼	cups water
450 g	2	(8-oz.) pkgs. refrigerator crescent rolls
110 g	¼	lb. Cheddar cheese, shredded
	1	small tomato, sliced

In a 10-inch skillet, brown ground beef and onion until beef loses redness; drain fat. Add Hunt's Tomato Paste, chili seasoning mix and water; simmer 6 to 8 minutes. Meanwhile, unroll crescent roll dough; separate into eight rectangles. Roll out or press each rectangle into square shape. Spoon equal amount of meat mixture onto each square; sprinkle generously with cheese and top with tomato slice. Fold corners of dough over filling to center so that all corners overlap. Place on ungreased cookie sheet. Bake at 375°F 20 minutes, or until golden brown. Makes 8 hot snacks.

Sopa de Albondigas

Meatball soup with a Spanish flair

450 g	1	lb. ground beef and pork for meat loaf
125 ml	½	cup seasoned dry bread crumbs
	1	egg
15 ml	1	Tablesp. chili powder
5 ml	1	teasp. salt
	10	pimiento-stuffed olives, halved
	1	medium onion, finely chopped
	2	cloves garlic, minced
30 ml	2	Tablesp. pure vegetable oil
170 g	1	(6-oz.) can Hunt's Tomato Paste
1125 ml	4½	cups water
	2	beef bouillon cubes
5 ml	1	teasp. oregano

In a bowl, combine ground meats, bread crumbs, egg, chili powder and salt. Form into 20 (1-inch) meatballs with an olive half in center of each. Sauté onion and garlic in oil in heavy kettle or Dutch oven until soft. Add Hunt's Tomato Paste, water, bouillon cubes and oregano. Heat to boiling. Add meatballs one at a time; reduce heat; cover; simmer 20 to 25 minutes. Makes 6 to 8 servings.

Lasagne Florentine

Creamy spinach and cheese filling sets this lasagne apart

225 g	8 ozs. lasagne noodles
450 g	1 lb. ground beef
	1 onion, chopped
	2 cloves garlic, minced
340 g	2 (6-oz.) or 1 (12-oz.) can Hunt's Tomato Paste
375 ml	1½ cups water
10 ml	2 teasp. salt
5 ml	1 teasp. basil
284 g	1 (10-oz.) pkg. frozen chopped spinach, thawed and pressed dry
225 g	8 ozs. ricotta or cottage cheese
	2 eggs, beaten
340 g	¾ lb. mozzarella cheese, shredded
60 ml	¼ cup grated Parmesan cheese

Cook noodles according to package directions; drain. In skillet, sauté ground beef, onion and garlic; drain fat. Stir in Hunt's Tomato Paste, water, *1 teaspoon* salt and basil; simmer 10 minutes. Meanwhile, in a bowl, combine spinach, ricotta and eggs. In 13 × 9 × 2-inch baking dish, spread ¼ *cup* meat mixture in thin layer; add layers of *half* the noodles, *all* the spinach and cheese mixture, *half* the mozzarella and *half* the meat mixture. Add remaining noodles, meat mixture and mozzarella in layers. Sprinkle with Parmesan. Bake at 350°F 30 minutes. Let stand 10 minutes before cutting. Makes 8 servings.

Down-Home Meat 'n Potatoes

Vegetables absorb the savory beef-tomato flavor

450 g	1 lb. ground beef
	1 onion, chopped
	1 clove garlic, crushed
170 g	1 (6-oz.) can Hunt's Tomato Paste
298 g	1 (10½-oz.) can beef broth
5 ml	1 teasp. salt
4 ml	¾ teasp. oregano
1 ml	¼ teasp. pepper
500 ml	2 cups thinly sliced potatoes
284 g	1 (10-oz.) pkg. frozen mixed vegetables, thawed
60 ml	¼ cup grated Parmesan cheese

In a skillet, brown beef with onion and garlic; drain fat. Stir in Hunt's Tomato Paste, broth, salt, oregano and pepper. In 2-quart casserole, layer meat mixture, potatoes and vegetables, beginning and ending with meat. Cover. Bake at 375°F 50 minutes. Uncover; bake 20 minutes longer. Sprinkle with cheese. Makes 6 servings.

Reach for Hunt's Tomato Paste

When Fish Is on the Menu . . .

When something is both as good and as good for you as seafood, you'll want to serve it often. Here are ways with low-fat, nutritious fish that enhance rather than disguise its delightful delicacy—that add heartiness and flavor that everyone will welcome. For great taste appeal, try Portuguese-style crab, a satisfying fish stew, Tuna Creole or any of the other recipes here.

Opposite: Mediterranean Fish Rolls (see page

Mediterranean Fish Rolls (Illustrated page 73)

Try this if you are counting calories

900 g	2	lbs. fillets of flounder, sole or perch
		Juice of ½ lemon
		Salt and pepper
60 ml	¼	cup chopped onion
	1	clove garlic, minced
30 ml	2	Tablesp. pure vegetable oil
170 g	1	(6-oz.) can Hunt's Tomato Paste
375ml	1½	cups water
1 ml	¼	teasp. oregano
60 ml	¼	cup dry white wine (optional)
		Lemon wedges
		Parsley

Cut fillets in half lengthwise. Sprinkle with lemon juice, salt and pepper. Roll up and fasten with toothpicks. Place in greased 10 × 6 × 2-inch baking dish. In a skillet, cook onion and garlic in oil until soft. Add Hunt's Tomato paste, water, ½ *teaspoon* salt, ¼ *teaspoon* pepper and oregano; mix well. Simmer, uncovered, 10 minutes. Add wine and pour over fish. Bake at 375°F 35 minutes or until fish flakes easily. Baste occasionally. Garnish with lemon wedges and parsley. Makes 6 servings.

Crab Portuguese

Truly unique and delicious flavor

	1	onion, chopped
	1	green pepper, sliced
30 ml	2	Tablesp. pure vegetable oil
170 g	1	(6-oz.) can Hunt's Tomato Paste
180 ml	¾	cup orange juice
125 ml	½	cup water
30 ml	2	Tablesp. sliced pimientos
15 ml	1	Tablesp. brown sugar, packed
5 ml	1	teasp. salt
340 g	12	ozs. cooked, canned or frozen crab
		Hot cooked rice
		Orange sections

In a skillet, cook onion and green pepper in oil until tender; stir in Hunt's Tomato Paste, orange juice, water, pimiento, brown sugar and salt. Simmer 10 minutes. Stir in crab; simmer only until crab is heated through. Serve over hot cooked rice; garnish with orange sections. Makes 6 servings.

Barbecued Red Snapper

Lime juice makes the sauce special

900 g	2	lbs. red snapper steaks or fillets
170 g	1	(6-oz.) can Hunt's Tomato Paste
85 ml	⅓	cup water
30 ml	2	Tablesp. lime juice
30 ml	2	Tablesp. Worcestershire
15 ml	1	Tablesp. sugar
15 ml	1	Tablesp. pure vegetable oil
5 ml	1	teasp. salt
.5 ml	⅛	teasp. garlic salt

Thaw fish if frozen; cut into serving-size portions. Combine remaining ingredients in a small bowl. Arrange fish on grill or broiler pan about 4 inches from heat source. Brush generously with sauce. Cook 6 to 10 minutes. Turn, brush with more sauce and cook 7 to 10 minutes longer or just until fish flakes when tested with a fork (length of cooking time depends on thickness of fish). Do not overcook. Makes 6 servings.

Tuna Creole in Rice Ring

Pretty and economical, too

	1	green pepper, chopped
125 ml	½	cup chopped onion
125 ml	½	cup sliced celery
	1	clove garlic, crushed
30 ml	2	Tablesp. pure vegetable oil
170 g	1	(6-oz.) can Hunt's Tomato Paste
310 ml	1¼	cups water
5 ml	1	teasp. salt
5 ml	1	teasp. dill weed
	1	bay leaf
		Dash Tabasco
400 g	2	(6½- to 7-oz.) cans chunk style tuna, drained and flaked
1000 ml	4	cups hot cooked rice

Sauté vegetables and garlic in oil until tender. Add Hunt's Tomato Paste, water and seasonings. Simmer 30 minutes, stirring occasionally. Stir in tuna; heat through. Pack hot cooked rice in buttered ring mold, turn out onto serving platter. Spoon tuna creole into center. Makes 4 servings.

Boatman's Stew

Mediterranean classic

900 g	2 lbs. firm-fleshed whitefish (cod, haddock or halibut), cut in large chunks
	Salt
	2 onions, sliced
30 ml	2 Tablesp. pure vegetable oil
170 g	1 (6-oz.) can Hunt's Tomato Paste
750 ml	3 cups water
1 ml	¼ teaspoon each: red pepper and black pepper
250 ml	1 cup finely chopped parsley
85 ml	⅓ cup dry white wine
	6 slices of Italian bread (toasted, if desired)

Sprinkle fish with ½ teaspoon salt; let stand 1 hour. Meanwhile, lightly brown onion in oil; pour off fat. Stir in Hunt's Tomato Paste, water, red pepper, 1½ teaspoons salt, black pepper, parsley and wine. Simmer 20 minutes. Add fish; simmer about 10 minutes longer or just until fish flakes easily with a fork. To serve, place a slice of bread in each soup bowl; ladle soup over. Makes 6 servings.

For perfect fish dishes . . . Cook fish *just* until it flakes apart easily with a fork.

Nice 'n Easy Jambalaya

Creole cooking at its best

375 ml	1½ cups diced ham
125 ml	½ cup chopped green pepper
125 ml	½ cup chopped onion
	1 clove garlic, minced
45 ml	3 Tablesp. pure vegetable oil
500 ml	2 cups water
170 g	1 (6-oz.) can Hunt's Tomato Paste
10 ml	2 teasp. brown sugar, packed
3 ml	½ teasp. Italian herb seasoning
3 ml	½ teasp. salt
250 ml	1 cup uncooked rice
375 ml	1½ cups cooked shrimp

In a large skillet, sauté ham, green pepper, onion and garlic in oil. Add water, Hunt's Tomato Paste, seasonings and rice; mix thoroughly. Bring to a boil. Simmer, tightly covered, 25 to 30 minutes. Add shrimp; heat through. Makes 6 to 8 servings.

Curried Shrimp Bake

Easy company dish

225 g	½	lb. bacon, cut in ½-inch pieces
125 ml	½	cup chopped onion
125 ml	½	cup chopped green pepper
675 g	1½	lbs. cooked or canned shrimp
125 ml	½	cup chopped peanuts
750 ml	3	cups cooked rice
170 g	1	(6-oz.) can Hunt's Tomato Paste
250 ml	1	cup sherry
370 g	1	(13-oz.) can evaporated milk
15 ml	1	Tablesp. lime juice
10 ml	2	teasp. curry powder
10 ml	2	teasp. Worcestershire
5 ml	1	teasp. salt

In a skillet, cook bacon until crisp; set aside. Cook onion and green pepper in bacon drippings until tender; drain fat. Thoroughly combine all remaining ingredients *except* bacon in a 9 × 13 × 2-inch baking dish; top with bacon. Bake at 350°F 45 minutes. Makes 8 to 9 servings.

Shrimp Risotto

Attractive one-dish dinner with Italian flair

	1	onion, chopped
250 ml	1	cup chopped green pepper
	1	clove garlic, minced
60 ml	¼	cup pure vegetable oil
250 ml	1	cup uncooked rice
170 g	1	(6-oz.) can Hunt's Tomato Paste
625 ml	2½	cups beef bouillon
3 ml	½	teasp. salt
1 ml	¼	teasp. basil
450 g	1	lb. raw shrimp. shelled and deveined
284 g	1	(10-oz.) pkg. frozen peas, thawed
110 g	1	(4-oz.) can sliced mushrooms, undrained
		Parsley

In a large skillet, cook onion, green pepper and garlic in oil until tender. Add rice; cook and stir until lightly browned. Stir in Hunt's Tomato Paste, bouillon, salt and basil; mix well. Cover tightly; simmer 30 to 35 minutes. Add shrimp, peas, mushrooms and liquid to rice mixture; cover and cook 15 minutes longer. Garnish with parsley. Makes 4 to 6 servings.

Reach for Hunt's Tomato Paste

When You'd Like to Serve a Special Salad or Vegetable . . .

When you plan a meal, you're most likely to settle on the main dish first and let the side dishes tag along, hoping for last-minute inspiration. Here are ways to make these orphans of the menu so delightful that they will be asked for again and again. There's a better-than-ever way to serve green beans, a zippy Mexican sauce you can use dozens of ways, and a tasty tomato-bacon salad dressing. Try each recipe—they're fun to make, fun to serve.

Opposite: Garbanzo Salad with Tangy Tomato-Herb Dressing (see page

Tangy Tomato-Herb Dressing

Delicious dressing for vegetable, meat or green salad

180 ml	¾ cup red wine vinegar
85 ml	⅓ cup brown sugar, packed
5 ml	1 teasp. onion powder
4 ml	¾ teasp. oregano
3 ml	½ teasp. <u>each</u>: celery seed, dill weed, paprika and salt
1 ml	¼ teasp. <u>each</u>: garlic powder and basil Dash pepper
310 ml	1¼ cups pure vegetable oil
170 g	1 (6-oz.) can Hunt's Tomato Paste

In a medium saucepan, bring vinegar, sugar and spices to a boil. Cool 10 minutes, add oil and Hunt's Tomato Paste. Stir or beat until creamy. Refrigerate. Mix before using. Makes 2⅔ cups.

For better bottled dressings . . . Add a tablespoon or two of tomato paste to Russian, Italian or French dressing for rich body, flavor and color.

Garbanzo Salad (Illustrated page 79)

425 g	1 (15-oz.) can garbanzo beans, drained
125 g	2 (2¼-oz.) cans sliced ripe olives, drained
250 ml	1 cup chopped green pepper
170 ml	⅔ cup chopped Bermuda onion
180 ml	¾ cup Tangy Tomato-Herb Dressing (recipe above)

Toss all ingredients, *except* dressing, in a large bowl. Add dressing and toss until well mixed. Cover; refrigerate 2 to 3 hours before serving. Makes 4 cups.

Vegetable Medley

Peanuts add crunch

	4 zucchini, sliced ¼ inch thick
170 ml	⅔ cup chopped onion
	1 clove garlic, minced
45 ml	3 Tablesp. butter or margarine
5 ml	1 teasp. oregano
3 ml	½ teasp. basil
3 ml	½ teasp. salt
	Dash pepper
450 g	1 (16-oz.) can whole kernel corn, drained
170 g	1 (6-oz.) can Hunt's Tomato Paste
85 ml	⅓ cup water
85 ml	⅓ cup chopped Spanish peanuts (optional)
170 ml	⅔ cup shredded sharp Cheddar cheese

Sauté zucchini, onion and garlic in butter in a large skillet or electric fry pan. When lightly browned, add seasonings. Stir in corn, Hunt's Tomato Paste and water. Cover; simmer 15 minutes or until zucchini is tender. Stir in all *but 1 tablespoon* of peanuts. Top with cheese; garnish with *remaining* peanuts. Cook 5 minutes longer to melt cheese. Makes 6 servings.

French Beans 'n Onions

Scrumptious side dish

	4 slices bacon, cut into ¼-inch pieces
	1 small onion, thinly sliced
450 g	16 ozs. frozen French-style green beans
125 ml	½ cup water
170 g	1 (6-oz.) can Hunt's Tomato Paste
15 ml	1 Tablesp. prepared mustard
3 ml	½ teasp. salt
	Dash pepper
125 ml	½ cup shredded Monterey Jack cheese

In a large skillet, brown bacon and onion; drain fat. Stir in beans and water. Cook, covered, over medium heat about 10 minutes. Thoroughly mix in remaining ingredients *except* cheese; simmer 5 minutes. Top with cheese and cook until melted. Makes 6 to 8 servings.

Mexicana Salsa

All-purpose sauce for Mexican dishes

170 g	1	(6-oz.) can Hunt's Tomato Paste
375 ml	1½	cups water
110 g	1	(4-oz.) can diced green chilies
60 ml	¼	cup finely chopped onion
8 ml	1 to 1½	teasp. chili powder
3 ml	½	teasp. sugar
3 ml	½	teasp. ground cumin
.5 ml	⅛	teasp. garlic powder
.5 ml	⅛	teasp. salt
		Dash pepper

Combine all ingredients in a medium saucepan; bring to a boil.
Simmer 10 to 15 minutes to blend flavors. Use as cooking or
serving sauce for vegetables, meats, eggs, tacos, tostadas,
enchiladas, casseroles or snack chips. Makes 2½ cups.

Eggplant Mexicana

	1	unpeeled eggplant, sliced ½ inch thick
675 ml	2½	cups Mexicana Salsa (recipe above)
250 ml	1	cup shredded sharp Cheddar cheese

Parboil eggplant slices 15 minutes or until tender; drain. Arrange in
a single layer in a buttered jelly roll pan. Cover eggplant slices with
Mexicana Salsa. Top each with cheese. Broil 10 minutes or until
cheese browns slightly. Makes 6 to 8 servings.

Avocado in Aspic

Handsome salad for a special meal

170 g	1	(6-oz.) pkg. lemon-flavored gelatin
500 ml	2	cups boiling water
170 g	1	(6-oz.) can Hunt's Tomato Paste
250 ml	1	cup cold water
15 ml	1	Tablesp. red wine vinegar
	2	ripe avocados, sliced lengthwise
60 ml	¼	cup chopped walnuts
	1	small onion, sliced in rings (optional)

In a 9-inch square glass dish, dissolve gelatin in *boiling* water. Add
Hunt's Tomato Paste, *cold* water and vinegar; mix thoroughly.
Arrange avocado slices in the gelatin; sprinkle with nuts.
Refrigerate until firm. To serve, cut into squares and garnish with
onion rings, if desired. Makes 9 to 12 servings.

Tomato-Bacon Dressing

Exceptional flavor for any green salad

170 g	1	(6-oz.) can Hunt's Tomato Paste
125 ml	½	cup water
90 ml	6	Tablesp. pure vegetable oil
60 ml	¼	cup red wine vinegar
	3	slices bacon, cooked and crumbled
15 ml	1	Tablesp. finely chopped onion
15 ml	1	Tablesp. sugar
1 ml	¼	teasp. celery seeds
1 ml	¼	teasp. marjoram
.5 ml	⅛	teasp. garlic powder
.5 ml	⅛	teasp. salt
		Dash pepper

In a medium bowl, mix Hunt's Tomato Paste, water, oil and vinegar until smooth. Stir in remaining ingredients. Refrigerate 2 to 3 hours to blend flavors. Mix well before using. Makes 1¾ cups.

Thousand Island Dressing

Never-fail all-time classic

250 ml	1	cup mayonnaise
170 g	1	(6-oz.) can Hunt's Tomato Paste
90 ml	6	Tablesp. water
15 ml	1	Tablesp. lemon juice
60 ml	¼	cup sweet pickle relish
3 ml	½	teasp. sugar
1 ml	¼	teasp. each: celery seeds, dill weed and onion powder
.5 ml	⅛	teasp. each: garlic powder and salt
		Dash pepper

In a medium bowl, mix mayonnaise, Hunt's Tomato Paste, water and lemon juice. Stir in *remaining* ingredients. Refrigerate 2 to 3 hours before serving. Makes 2½ cups.

Quick Sour Cream Dressing

250 ml	1	cup sour cream
30 ml	2	Tablesp. Hunt's Tomato Paste
15 ml	1 to 2	Tablesp. milk
10 ml	2	teasp. minced capers (optional)
3 ml	½	teasp. salt
1 ml	¼	teasp. basil, crushed

In a small bowl, thoroughly blend all ingredients; chill. Serve over hot or chilled cooked vegetables, coleslaw or potato salad. Makes 1½ cups.

Reach for Hunt's Tomato Paste

When You've Invited Company . . .

You want to serve something special—but you also want to have time to enjoy your own party. Here is a collection of just-right recipes. There's double-duty Rumaki, for example, that can serve as either appetizer or entrée. There's a great Paella, a version of Beef Wellington that won't break your budget, some very special meatballs, lots more. So get started—make up the menu, invite the guests!

Opposite: Ratatouille Crèpes (see page 8

Ratatouille Crèpes (Illustrated page 85)

Whisper-thin pancakes enclose a savory vegetable medley

	3 zucchini, sliced
	2 crookneck squash, sliced
	10 mushrooms, sliced
	1 onion, sliced
	1 green pepper, cut in strips
	1 clove garlic, minced
45 ml	3 Tablesp. pure vegetable oil
170 g	1 (6-oz.) can Hunt's Tomato Paste
	Water
30 ml	2 Tablesp. chopped pimientos
5 ml	1 teasp. salt
5 ml	1 teasp. Italian herb seasoning
1 ml	¼ teasp. pepper
	14 to 16 crèpes (recipe follows)
	Chopped parsley

In a skillet, sauté zucchini, crookneck, mushrooms, onion, green pepper and garlic in oil until vegetables are limp. Stir in Hunt's Tomato Paste, *one* can water, pimiento, salt, Italian herb seasoning and pepper. Simmer 10 to 15 minutes. Place about *3 tablespoons* of vegetable mixture down center of each crèpe; fold sides to overlap. Place on serving plates, allowing 2 per serving. Spoon remaining mixture over folded crèpes. Top with chopped parsley. Makes 7 to 8 servings.

Crèpes: In a blender container, combine ⅔ *cup each:* milk and water, 2 *whole* eggs and 1 egg *yolk;* add 1¼ *cups sifted* all-purpose flour, ¼ *teaspoon* salt and 2 *tablespoons* melted butter; blend. Heat 8-inch crèpe pan over high heat. Remove pan from heat; brush lightly with melted butter. Pour in a *scant 3 tablespoons* batter, tilting pan to thinly coat bottom. Return to heat. When crèpe is lightly browned, turn and brown other side. Makes 14 to 16 crèpes.

To serve as entrée crèpes ...add 2 to 3 tablespoons shredded Cheddar cheese to the filling in each crèpe. Top servings with additional shredded cheese; place under broiler a few moments to melt cheese.

Stuffed Flank Steak Roll

Flank steak at its flavorful best

675 g	1	flank steak (about 1½ lbs.), butterflied
170 g	1	(6-oz.) can Hunt's Tomato Paste
625 ml	2½	cups water
30 ml	2	Tablesp. chili powder
10 ml	2	teasp. salt
5 ml	1	teasp. garlic powder
3 ml	½	teasp. ground cumin
1 ml	¼	teasp. Tabasco
225 g	½	lb. Italian sausage
	1	onion, chopped
110 g	1	(4-oz.) can diced green chilies
30 ml	2	Tablesp. sliced ripe olives
15 ml	1	Tablesp. sliced pimientos
500 ml	2	cups corn bread crumbs

Pound steak with a meat mallet to about ⅛-inch thickness. Combine Hunt's Tomato Paste, water, chili powder, *1 teaspoon* salt, garlic powder, cumin and Tabasco. In a shallow baking dish, marinate flank steak in tomato paste mixture about 1 hour. Meanwhile, sauté Italian sausage and onion in skillet; drain fat; remove from heat. Drain steak; *reserve* marinade. Stir *¾ cup* marinade and remaining ingredients *except* steak into mixture in skillet. Spread mixture over entire surface of steak. Starting with either cut end, roll steak jelly-roll fashion with the grain. Secure with toothpicks or kitchen string. Place in shallow baking dish. Bake at 375°F 1 to 1½ hours, basting often. Makes 6 to 8 servings.

Glazed Ham and Fruit

Try this spicy glaze on fresh pork roast, too

170 g	1	(6-oz.) can Hunt's Tomato Paste
250 ml	1	cup water
60 ml	¼	cup vinegar
125 ml	½	cup brown sugar, packed
45 ml	3	Tablesp. orange juice
8 ml	1½	teasp. grated orange rind
5 ml	1	teasp. each: ground cloves and cinnamon
	3	lb. cooked boneless ham
		Peach halves or pineapple rings

In a small bowl, thoroughly combine *first 8* ingredients. Place ham in shallow baking dish. Arrange fruit around ham. Spoon glaze mixture over ham and fruit. Bake at 375°F 1 hour, basting often. Makes 8 to 10 servings.

Paella

One of Spain's wonderful contributions to dining pleasure

1350 g	1	(2½- to 3-lb.) frying chicken, cut up
60 ml	¼	cup pure vegetable oil
	1	onion, sliced
	2	cloves garlic, minced
170 g	1	(6-oz.) can Hunt's Tomato Paste
		Water
		Salt
1 ml	¼	teasp. dried saffron
250 ml	1	cup uncooked rice
3 ml	½	teasp. oregano
450 g	1	lb. raw shrimp, shelled and cleaned
196 g	1	(6½- to 7-oz.) can whole clams, drained
284 g	1	(10-oz.) pkg. frozen peas, thawed
110 g	1	(4-oz.) can pimiento strips

In a Dutch oven or heavy kettle, brown chicken in oil; add onion and garlic, sauté until limp; drain fat. Combine Hunt's Tomato Paste, *2 cups* water and *1 teaspoon* salt; pour over chicken. Simmer, covered, 20 minutes. Stir saffron into *1 cup* boiling water; add to chicken. Stir in rice, oregano and *1 teaspoon* salt. Simmer, covered, 35 minutes. Add shrimp, clams, peas and pimiento; cook 10 minutes longer, stirring occasionally. Makes 8 servings.

Fondue

The perfect way to entertain informally

450 g	1	lb. large raw shrimp, shelled and cleaned
450 g	1	lb. beef sirloin tip, cut in bite-size cubes
450 g	1	lb. boneless chicken breast, cut in bite-size pieces
	4	large zucchini, sliced in 1-inch pieces
750 ml	3	cups pure vegetable oil
		Bamboo skewers or fondue forks
		Spicy Dipping Sauce (recipe follows)

Arrange shrimp, beef, chicken and zucchini on a serving platter; refrigerate until ready to cook. Heat oil in 1½-quart heavy saucepan or fondue pot to 375°F. Allow guests to spear meats and zucchini on skewers or fondue forks; immerse in hot oil from 30 seconds to a minute, cooking to desired doneness. Dip in Spicy Dipping Sauce. Makes 8 servings.

Spicy Dipping Sauce: In a 1-quart saucepan, combine 1 (6-oz.) can Hunt's Tomato Paste, 1½ *cups* water, *2 tablespoons each*: grated onion, lemon juice and chopped parsley, *1 clove* garlic, crushed. Simmer 20 minutes. Stir in ½ *cup* sour cream and 2 teaspoons *each*: chives and dill seeds. Makes 2 cups sauce.

Caution: overheating any oil may cause fire. Reduce heat if oil smokes.

Mock Beef Wellington

Juicy, flavorful meat loaf, party dressed in flaky pastry

170 g	1 (6-oz.) can Hunt's Tomato Paste
250 ml	1 cup water
900 g	2 lbs. extra-lean ground beef
250 ml	1 cup fine dry bread crumbs
	1 egg, separated
30 ml	2 Tablesp. prepared horseradish
5 ml	1 teasp. salt
3 ml	½ teasp. monosodium glutamate
	1 pie crust stick
	Wine Sauce (recipe follows)

In a saucepan, blend together Hunt's Tomato Paste and water. In a bowl, combine ½ cup tomato paste mixture with ground beef, bread crumbs, egg *yolk*, horseradish, salt and monosodium glutamate. Shape mixture into rectangular loaf. Bake on rack in shallow baking pan at *375°F* 45 minutes. Meanwhile, prepare pie crust stick according to package directions. Roll into rectangle large enough to wrap loaf; place loaf on pastry. Wrap pastry around loaf, overlapping edges on bottom. Trim off excess pastry. Moisten edges and pinch together to seal. Make decorative cut-outs from excess pastry and arrange on top of loaf. Place on ungreased baking pan. Brush lightly with beaten egg *white*. Bake at *400°F* 20 minutes longer. Slice and serve with Wine Sauce. Makes 6 to 8 servings.

Wine Sauce: Add ¼ *cup* wine, *2 tablespoons each*: brown sugar, lemon juice and Worcestershire and ¼ *teaspoon* crushed tarragon to remaining tomato paste mixture in saucepan. Simmer over low heat 10 minutes. Makes about 1½ cups sauce.

Italian Sandwich Pockets

A quick supper when friends drop by

450 g	1 lb. Italian sausage, cut in 1-inch pieces
	1 onion, sliced
	1 green pepper, cut in strips
	5 large mushrooms, sliced
170 g	1 (6-oz.) can Hunt's Tomato Paste
375 ml	1½ cups water
42 g	1 (1½-oz.) pkg. spaghetti sauce mix
	6 small rounds pita or Arabic bread

In a skillet, sauté Italian sausage, onion, green pepper and mushrooms until sausage loses its redness. Stir in Hunt's Tomato Paste, water and spaghetti sauce mix. Blend well. Simmer 10 to 15 minutes. Split pita rounds in half. Fill each half with equal portions of sausage mixture. Makes 6 servings.

Hearty Skillet Omelet

A meatless wonder for Sunday brunch

170 g	1	(6-oz.) jar marinated artichoke hearts, drained
250 ml	1	cup sliced mushrooms
45 ml	3	Tablesp. butter
	6	eggs
30 ml	2	Tablesp. water
5 ml	1	teasp. seasoned salt
3 ml	½	teasp. coarse ground pepper
250 ml	1	cup shredded Swiss cheese
		Spicy Mexican Sauce (recipe follows)

In a 10-inch ovenproof skillet, sauté artichoke hearts and mushrooms in butter, tilting pan to coat sides and bottom. In a bowl, beat eggs with water, salt and pepper; pour over mushrooms and artichokes. Stir lightly to mix. As mixture cooks, loosen edges with spatula and tilt pan to let uncooked portion run under until omelet is set. Sprinkle with cheese; place under broiler until cheese melts and omelet is browned. Serve wedges topped with Spicy Mexican Sauce. Makes 6 servings.

Spicy Mexican Sauce: Sauté ½ cup chopped green onion and 1 clove garlic, crushed, in saucepan in 1 tablespoon pure vegetable oil. Stir in 1 (6-oz.) can Hunt's Tomato Paste, 1½ cups water, 1 teaspoon each: Italian herb seasoning, seasoned salt and 1 beef bouillon cube. Simmer 5 to 10 minutes. Makes 2 cups sauce.

Rumaki

Spicy marinade makes liver and bacon special

125 ml	½	cup ketchup
60 ml	¼	cup Hunt's Tomato Paste
310 ml	1¼	cups water
30 ml	2	Tablesp. Worcestershire
5 ml	1	teasp. seasoned salt
1 ml	¼	teasp. Tabasco
450 g	1	lb. chicken livers, cut in half
	12	slices bacon, cut in half

Combine first 6 ingredients in mixing bowl. Add livers; stir to coat. Let stand 20 minutes. Drain, reserving marinade. Wrap each liver piece in half strip of bacon; secure with toothpicks. Broil on rack about 2 inches from source of heat about 10 minutes, turning often. Heat reserved marinade in small saucepan to boil; simmer 2 minutes. Use as dip for Rumaki. Makes 4 entrée servings or about 24 hors d'oeuvres.

Reach for Hunt's Tomato Paste

When Everyone's Asking for Snacks . . .

Snacking's not about to go out of style, whether it's after school, quick lunches or company hors d'oeuvres. The trick is to provide good snacks—tasty, nutritious ones that provide more than empty calories. Pizza tops almost everyone's list, so here is a from-scratch pizza, a shortcut version and tasty mini-pizzas. But that's only for starters—there's lots more for contented munching any time of the day.

Opposite: Teriyaki Kabobs (see page

Teriyaki Kabobs (Illustrated page 93)

An elegant appetizer

125 ml	½	cup soy sauce
125 ml	½	cup honey
60 ml	¼	cup cream sherry
170 g	1	(6-oz.) can Hunt's Tomato Paste
125 ml	½	cup water
5 ml	1	teasp. grated orange rind
3 ml	½	teasp. salt
3 ml	½	teasp. garlic powder
900 g	2	lbs. sirloin steak, cut in 20 cubes
	20	large raw shrimp, shelled and cleaned
560 g	1	(20-oz.) can pineapple chunks, drained
	5	green onions, cut into 2-inch pieces
	1	large green pepper, cut into 1-inch squares
	20	(6-inch) skewers

In a large bowl, combine *first 8* ingredients; mix thoroughly. Add beef and shrimp; cover and refrigerate at least 3 hours. Drain beef and shrimp, reserving marinade. To assemble kabobs, place cube of meat, shrimp, pineapple chunk, green onion piece and green pepper square on each skewer. Place skewers on rack in broiling pan; brush with reserved marinade. Broil 5 inches from heat 3 to 5 minutes or until meat is brown and shrimp is pink; turn and brush with marinade; broil 5 minutes longer. Makes 20 kabobs.

Hurry-Up Pepperoni Pizza

Refrigerated dough is the secret

170 g	1	(6-oz.) can Hunt's Tomato Paste
310 ml	1¼	cups water
85 ml	⅓	cup grated Parmesan cheese
15 ml	1	Tablesp. olive oil
10 ml	2	teasp. Italian herb seasoning
3 ml	½	teasp. salt
3 ml	½	teasp. sugar
450 g	2	(8-oz.) pkgs. refrigerator crescent rolls
375 ml	1½	cups shredded mozzarella cheese
		Pepperoni slices

In a small bowl, combine *first 7* ingredients; set aside. Meanwhile, on lightly floured board, roll out crescent roll dough to fit jelly roll pan. Spoon tomato paste mixture onto dough. Top with cheese and pepperoni. Bake at 450°F 10 to 12 minutes or until crust is golden brown. Makes 1 (11 × 14-inch) pizza.

Tostada Carne

Open-face sandwich, Mexican style

	8	corn tortillas
		Pure vegetable oil
450 g	1	lb. lean ground beef
125 ml	½	cup chopped onion
170 g	1	(6-oz.) can Hunt's Tomato Paste
375 ml	1½	cups water
35 g	1	(1¼-oz.) env. taco seasoning mix
560 g	1	(1-lb. 4-oz.) can refried beans
500 ml	2	cups shredded Cheddar cheese
500 ml	2	cups shredded lettuce
	1	medium tomato, chopped

In a skillet, over medium-high heat, fry tortillas one at a time in 1 inch of oil 1 to 2 minutes or until slightly crisp. Drain on paper towels. Sauté ground beef and onion in a 10-inch skillet; drain excess fat. Add Hunt's Tomato Paste, water and taco seasoning mix; simmer 8 to 10 minutes. Meanwhile, heat beans and ½ *cup* cheese in saucepan or double boiler until cheese is melted; stir often. To assemble tostadas, spread each tortilla with equal portion of beans and meat mixture. Sprinkle each with lettuce and *remaining* cheese; top with tomatoes. Makes 8 tostadas.

Speedy Mini-Pizzas

English muffins make an "instant" crust

170 g	1	(6-oz.) can Hunt's Tomato Paste
250 ml	1	cup water
60 ml	¼	cup grated Parmesan cheese
1 ml	¼	teasp. oregano
1 ml	¼	teasp. sugar
	6	English muffins, split and toasted
225 g	8	ozs. shredded mozzarella cheese
		Toppings: sliced pepperoni, green pepper rings, sliced olives, sliced mushrooms

In a small bowl, combine Hunt's Tomato Paste, water, Parmesan, oregano and sugar. Spread equal amounts on muffin halves. Sprinkle with mozzarella; garnish with toppings as desired. Broil 3 to 4 minutes or until cheese melts. Makes 12 mini-pizzas.

Seafood Cocktail Sauce

The perfect complement to shrimp or crab

170 g	1	(6-oz.) can Hunt's Tomato Paste
250 ml	1	cup water
5 ml	1	teasp. Worcestershire
60 ml	¼	cup minced pickle or pickle relish
10 ml	2	teasp. lemon juice
5 ml	1	teasp. horseradish
3 ml	½	teasp. salt
1 ml	¼	teasp. sugar
.5 ml	⅛	teasp. pepper

Combine all ingredients in a bowl. Chill thoroughly to blend flavors. Serve with crab, shrimp or mixed seafood cocktail. Makes 1½ cups.

Another way: Mix this sauce half-and-half with mayonnaise; use to dress any kind of seafood salad.

Cheesy Tortilla Chips with Salsa

Restaurants call these Nachos

170 g	1	(6-oz.) can Hunt's Tomato Paste
250 ml	1	cup water
110 g	1	(4-oz.) can diced green chilies
125 ml	½	cup <u>each</u>: finely chopped onion and green pepper
10 ml	2	teasp. lemon juice
1 ml	¼	teasp. Tabasco
250 g	1	(9-oz.) bag tortilla chips
500 ml	2	cups Cheddar cheese, shredded

To make salsa, combine Hunt's Tomato Paste, water, *half* the green chilies, onion, green pepper, lemon juice and Tabasco in a small bowl; mix thoroughly. Let stand about 30 minutes. Just before serving, spread tortilla chips in a single layer on jelly roll pans or cookie sheets. Sprinkle with cheese and remaining chilies; broil for 3 minutes or until cheese melts. Serve tortilla chips with salsa as a dip. Makes 6 to 8 servings.

Hot Bean Dip

Truly a dipper's delight

560 g	1	(1-lb. 4-oz.) can refried beans
110 g	1	(4-oz.) can diced green chilies
225 g	½	lb. Cheddar cheese, shredded
125 ml	½	cup minced onion
45 ml	3	Tablesp. Hunt's Tomato Paste
	5	to 6 drops Tabasco
30 ml	2	Tablesp. chopped pimientos

In a 1½-quart saucepan, combine all ingredients. Heat over low heat, stirring constantly, until cheese is melted and mixture is hot. Serve in chafing dish with tortilla chips. Makes 2½ cups.

Coney Island Chili Dogs

Their fame has spread 'round the world

225 g	½	lb. lean ground beef
250 ml	1	cup chopped onion
170 g	1	(6-oz.) can Hunt's Tomato Paste
250 ml	1	cup water
30 ml	2	Tablesp. chili powder
5 ml	1	teasp. salt
3 ml	½	teasp. garlic powder
3 ml	½	teasp. ground cumin
1 ml	¼	teasp. sugar
450 g	1	lb. hot dogs
	10	hot dog buns
250 ml	1	cup shredded Cheddar cheese (optional)

In a 10-inch skillet, brown beef and onion until beef loses redness. Stir in Hunt's Tomato Paste, water and seasonings; heat through. Meanwhile, heat or grill hot dogs and buns. To serve, place hot dogs in buns; spoon chili down center of each; top with shredded cheese. Makes 10 chili dogs.

Coney Island Chili Dogs
Oven French Fries
Relish Cups
Milk
Make-Your-Own
Sundaes

Sloppy Joe Pizza

Two favorites in one

390 g	1	(13¾-oz.) pkg. hot roll mix
450 g	1	lb. ground beef
3 ml	½	teasp. <u>each</u>: salt and Italian herb seasoning
42 g	1	(1½-oz.) env. seasoning mix for sloppy joes
170 g	1	(6-oz.) can Hunt's Tomato Paste
180 ml	¾	cup water
225 g	8	ozs. mozzarella cheese, shredded
		Sliced ripe olives
		Onion rings, thinly sliced

Prepare hot roll mix for pizza dough according to package directions, using *1 cup warm water*. Roll out to fit a greased jelly roll pan. Bake at 450°F 5 minutes; set aside. Meanwhile, sauté ground beef lightly in skillet; add salt, Italian herb seasoning, sloppy joe mix, Hunt's Tomato Paste and water. Simmer 5 to 10 minutes. Spread over partially baked crust. Top with mozzarella, olives and onion rings. Bake at 450°F 20 minutes. Cut into squares. Makes 8 to 10 servings.

Pizza Sauce

Tomato paste for body and deep-down good taste

125 ml	½	cup finely chopped onion
30 ml	2	Tablesp. pure vegetable oil
	2	cloves garlic, minced
170 g	1	(6-oz.) can Hunt's Tomato Paste
625 ml	2½	cups water
8 ml	1½	teasp. oregano
5 ml	1	teasp. salt
5 ml	1	teasp. sugar
3 ml	½	teasp. basil
	1	bay leaf
		Dash pepper

In a 1½-quart saucepan, sauté onion in oil until golden. Add garlic; cook 1 or 2 minutes longer, stirring. Add remaining ingredients; simmer slowly, uncovered, about 1 hour or until thick. Remove bay leaf. Makes 2 cups sauce; enough for 2 (15-inch) pizzas.

Barbecued Cocktail Franks

Savory hurry-up appetizers

170 g	1 (6-oz.) can Hunt's Tomato Paste
500 ml	2 cups water
30 ml	2 Tablesp. each: minced onion, Worcestershire and brown sugar
15 ml	1 Tablesp. each: white vinegar and molasses
5 ml	1 teasp. each: lemon juice and dry mustard
3 ml	½ teasp. salt
450 g	1 lb. cocktail frankfurters

In a large saucepan, combine all ingredients *except* frankfurters. Bring to boil, stirring frequently; reduce heat. Add franks; simmer 10 minutes. Serve with toothpicks. Makes 32 appetizers.

To keep these hot . . . Serve in a fondue pot, electric skillet or chafing dish.

Sesame Seed Chicken Wings

Serve warm from a chafing dish

	12 chicken wings
30 ml	2 Tablesp. pure vegetable oil
170 g	1 (6-oz.) can Hunt's Tomato Paste
375 ml	1½ cups beef broth
30 ml	2 Tablesp. sesame seeds, toasted
8 ml	1½ teasp. paprika
5 ml	1 teasp. sage
5 ml	1 teasp. salt

Remove tips from wings; separate at joint. Brown wing pieces lightly in oil in skillet. Combine remaining ingredients in a 1½-quart glass baking dish; blend well. Add chicken wings; turn to coat. Let stand 2 hours. Bake, uncovered, at 375°F 35 to 40 minutes. Makes 24 appetizers.

Chilies con Queso

Zesty cheese dip

225 g	½ lb. process American cheese, cut into ½-inch cubes
170 g	1 (6-oz.) can Hunt's Tomato Paste
250 ml	1 cup water
110 g	1 (4-oz.) can diced green chilies
125 ml	½ cup minced onion
60 ml	¼ cup diced green pepper
10 ml	2 teasp. lemon juice
1 ml	¼ teasp. Tabasco
	Tortilla or corn chips

In a saucepan, melt cheese over low heat. Meanwhile, combine remaining ingredients *except* tortilla chips in a small bowl; stir into melted cheese. Serve in fondue pot or chafing dish with tortilla chips. Makes 1 quart.

Pizza from Scratch

Homemade is best of all

1000 ml	3½ to 4 cups sifted all-purpose flour
	2 pkgs. active dry yeast
375 ml	1½ cups water
45 ml	3 Tablesp. olive or pure vegetable oil
13 ml	2½ teasp. salt
	Pizza Sauce (see pg. 99)
750 ml	3 cups shredded mozzarella, jack or Cheddar cheese
	Toppings: prosciutto ham, pepperoni, salami, Italian sausage, tiny meatballs, anchovies, shrimp, capers, green pepper, onion rings, mushrooms

In a large mixer bowl, combine *2 cups* flour and yeast. In a saucepan, blend water, oil and salt; heat to lukewarm (120 to 130°F). Add to flour mixture; beat on medium speed 3 minutes. Stir in 1½ *to 2 cups more* flour to make a stiff dough. Knead on floured board until smooth. Place in greased bowl; turn once to grease entire surface. Cover and let rise (about 1 hour) until double. Punch down; let rest 10 minutes. Form into 2 balls. Roll each to fit a 15-inch pizza or jelly roll pan. Place in pans and form edges. Prick crusts. Bake at 450°F 15 to 20 minutes. Spread Pizza Sauce over surfaces. Sprinkle with shredded cheese; add desired toppings. Bake 10 minutes longer. Makes 2 (15-inch) pizzas.

Reach for Hunt's Tomato Paste

When You Want to Try Something New . . .

Do you have days when you look around the kitchen and suddenly feel a wave of creativity coming over you? Then this section is for you, a collection of never-before incredible edibles, all of them absolutely delicious. Recipes for a chocolate cake that keeps beautifully (if you can hide it from snackers), a zesty Bloody Mary mix, even a relish that's sure to please. Be creative!

Opposite: Pennsylvania Dutch Tomato Pie (see page 10

Pennsylvania Dutch Tomato Pie

(Illustrated page 103)

Farm-style rich and delicious

	4	eggs
170 g	1	(6-oz.) can Hunt's Tomato Paste
750 ml	3	cups brown sugar, packed
125 ml	½	cup milk
10 ml	2	teasp. vanilla
	1	unbaked 9-inch pie shell
60 g	1	(2⅛-oz.) pkg. pecan pieces (optional)

Place eggs in a large bowl; beat slightly with hand or electric beater. Add Hunt's Tomato Paste, brown sugar, milk and vanilla; beat until just blended. Pour into pie shell. Bake at 425°F 15 minutes, *reduce heat* to 350°F, bake 30 to 40 minutes longer until set. If desired, sprinkle with pecan pieces. Makes 8 servings.

Saucy Vegetable Topper

Even confirmed vegetable-haters will ask for seconds

45 ml	3	Tablesp. butter or margarine
30 ml	2	Tablesp. flour
310 ml	1¼	cups water
60 ml	¼	cup Hunt's Tomato Paste
30 ml	2	Tablesp. grated Parmesan cheese
3 ml	½	teasp. onion powder
3 ml	½	teasp. tarragon
1 ml	¼	teasp. salt
.5 ml	⅛	teasp. garlic powder
		Dash pepper

In a medium saucepan, melt butter; add flour. Cook over low heat, stirring, until bubbly. Blend in water and Hunt's Tomato Paste until smooth. Add remaining ingredients; bring to boil. Simmer 5 to 10 minutes, stirring occasionally. Serve over hot cooked broccoli, cauliflower or other vegetable. Makes 2½ cups.

Piccadilly Rarebit

Top with crisp bacon slices to make this special

170 g	1	(6-oz.) can Hunt's Tomato Paste
180 ml	¾	cup beer
560 g	1¼	lbs. sharp Cheddar cheese, shredded
3 ml	½	teasp. onion powder
	4	English muffins, split and toasted

In a medium saucepan, combine Hunt's Tomato Paste and beer; heat to boiling. Add cheese and onion powder. Lower heat and cook, stirring, until cheese is melted. *Do not boil.* Serve over muffin halves. Makes 4 servings.

Bloody Mary Mix

Excellent body, splendid flavor

340 g	2	(6-oz.) or 1 (12-oz.) can Hunt's Tomato Paste
1000 ml	1	qt. water
60 ml	¼	cup lemon juice
10 ml	2	teasp. Worcestershire
5 ml	1	teasp. salt
3 ml	½	teasp. each: sugar and onion powder
1 ml	¼	teasp. celery salt
1 ml	¼	teasp. Tabasco

Combine all ingredients in a 2-quart container with a tight-fitting cover; shake to blend well. Chill at least 1 hour. Makes about 6 cups.

To make a Bloody Mary: Fill 10-ounce glass with ice cubes. Add *2 ounces* vodka. Fill glass with Bloody Mary Mix; stir and serve.

To use as a non-alcoholic tomato cocktail: Shake Bloody Mary Mix with an additional *1 cup* water. Pour into glasses over ice cubes. Serve with celery-stick stirrer or lemon wedge, if desired.

Spicy Tomato Relish

Excellent relish for meat dishes

170 g	1	(6-oz.) can Hunt's Tomato Paste
125 ml	½	cup water
85 ml	⅓	cup brown sugar, packed
60 ml	¼	cup red wine vinegar
15 ml	1	Tablesp. prepared mustard
15 ml	1	Tablesp. prepared horseradish
4 ml	¾	teasp. salt
3 ml	½	teasp. cinnamon
.5 ml	⅛	teasp. mace
.5 ml	⅛	teasp. ground cloves
410 g	1	(14½-oz.) can Hunt's Whole Tomatoes, drained and finely chopped
125 ml	½	cup finely chopped celery
60 ml	¼	cup finely chopped onion
	1	apple, finely chopped

In a medium bowl, combine all ingredients *except* chopped vegetables and apple. Mix until smooth. Stir in tomato, celery, onion and apple. Refrigerate 2 to 3 hours before serving. Makes 4 cups.

Red Rover Jumbles

Soft, spicy, grandmother-type cookies

1180 ml	4¾ cups all-purpose flour
5 ml	1 teasp. <u>each</u>: baking soda, cinnamon and ginger
3 ml	½ teasp. <u>each</u>: ground cloves and salt
250 ml	1 cup shortening
310 ml	1¼ cups sugar
	2 eggs
250 ml	1 cup molasses
170 g	1 (6-oz.) can Hunt's Tomato Paste
170 ml	⅔ cup buttermilk
500 ml	2 cups raisins

Sift together flour, soda, spices and salt; reserve. In a bowl, beat shortening and sugar until well blended; beat in eggs. Add molasses. Combine Hunt's Tomato Paste and buttermilk; add alternately with flour mixture. Stir until well blended. Stir in raisins. Drop by rounded teaspoonfuls onto greased baking sheets. Bake at 375°F 10 minutes. Cool; store tightly covered. Makes about 8 dozen.

Brownie Drops

Just right for the munching set

310 ml	1¼ cups sugar
170 ml	⅔ cup butter or margarine
	2 eggs, beaten
170 g	1 (6-oz.) can Hunt's Tomato Paste
170 g	1 (6-oz.) pkg. semisweet chocolate morsels, melted
750 ml	3 cups sifted all-purpose flour
10 ml	2 teasp. baking powder
4 ml	¾ teasp. cinnamon
1 ml	¼ teasp. baking soda
1 ml	¼ teasp. salt
250 ml	1 cup chopped walnuts

Cream sugar and butter in a large bowl. Beat in eggs. Add Hunt's Tomato Paste and melted chocolate, mix thoroughly. In another bowl, sift together flour, baking powder, cinnamon, baking soda and salt. Stir into chocolate mixture; mix well. Stir in walnuts. Drop by rounded teaspoonfuls 2 inches apart onto greased baking sheets. Bake at 375°F 12 to 15 minutes. Makes 5½ to 6 dozen cookies.

Quick Mahogany Cake

Rich, wonderful chocolate-plus flavor

	1	(2-layer size) pkg. devil's food cake mix
	1	(4-serving size) pkg. chocolate instant pudding mix
170 g	1	(6-oz.) can Hunt's Tomato Paste
180 ml	¾	cup water
	4	eggs
125 ml	½	cup pure vegetable oil
15 ml	1	Tablesp. instant coffee powder
3 ml	½	teasp. cinnamon
		Confectioner's sugar

Combine all ingredients in large bowl of electric mixer. Beat at low speed until well blended; beat at medium speed 2 minutes, scraping bowl several times. Turn into greased 10-inch tube pan. Bake at 350°F 50 to 55 minutes, or until cake springs back when pressed with fingertip. Cool on wire rack 15 minutes. Remove from pan, complete cooling on rack. Sprinkle lightly with confectioner's sugar before cutting. Makes 12 to 16 servings.

Baked Noodle Pudding

Conversation piece as a side dish or unique dessert

225 g	1	(8-oz.) pkg. wide noodles
125 ml	½	cup raisins
125 ml	½	cup chopped prunes
60 ml	¼	cup chopped nuts
	3	eggs, well beaten
250 ml	1	cup sour cream
30 ml	2	Tablesp. Hunt's Tomato Paste
125 ml	½	cup water
60 ml	¼	cup brown sugar, packed
1 ml	¼	teasp. cinnamon
60 ml	¼	cup butter or margarine
60 ml	¼	cup dry bread crumbs

Cook noodles according to package directions. Drain and rinse with hot water. Combine noodles, raisins, prunes and nuts in a large bowl. In a small bowl, beat eggs with sour cream, Hunt's Tomato Paste, water, sugar and cinnamon. Add to noodle mixture and toss to blend. Melt butter in a 1½-quart casserole. Pour noodle mixture into casserole. Sprinkle crumbs over top. Bake at 350°F 30 to 35 minutes or until pudding is lightly browned on top. For dessert, serve with whipped cream. Makes 6 to 8 servings.

Reach for Hunt's Tomato Paste

When You're Cooking for a Crowd . . .

Making a special dish for a holiday gathering, the food bazaar or the church supper can be a challenge. It must be easy to prepare and serve, but also hearty and satisfying. Here is a wide variety of just such dishes that will satisfy both the eye and the appetite. You'll find some wonderful chicken specialties, barbecue sauce by the bucket, and a bonanza of great casseroles. What's more, none of these will cost more time, effort or money than you'll want to spend.

Opposite: Sloppy Joes for 75 (see page 110)

Sloppy Joes for 75 (Illustrated page 109)

Onion soup mix is the flavor trick

4500 g	10	lbs. lean ground beef
	9	stalks celery, chopped
850 g	5	(6-oz.) cans Hunt's Tomato Paste
1250 ml	5	cups water
	3	env. dry onion soup mix
560 g	1	(20-oz.) bottle ketchup
60 ml	¼	cup prepared mustard
60 ml	¼	cup brown sugar, packed
15 ml	1	Tablesp. seasoned salt
8 ml	1½	teasp. pepper
	75	hamburger buns

Cook beef and celery in 12-quart or larger kettle until beef loses redness; drain fat. Stir in remaining ingredients, *except buns;* blend well. Simmer 15 to 20 minutes, stirring occasionally, until desired consistency. Serve on toasted or plain buns. Makes about 75 (⅓ cup) servings.

To round out the flavors . . .
Add a teaspoon of white or brown sugar to your tomato paste dishes.

Hunt's Chili-Mac

Kids love this

1800 g	4	lbs. ground beef
500 ml	2	cups chopped onion
500 ml	2	cups chopped celery
1190 g	7	(6-oz.) cans Hunt's Tomato Paste
2000 ml	2	qts. water
60 ml	¼	cup brown sugar, packed
30 ml	2	Tablesp. vinegar
23 ml	1½	Tablesp. salt
23 ml	1½	Tablesp. chili powder
15 ml	1	Tablesp. prepared mustard
1500 ml	6	cups shredded Cheddar cheese
900 g	2	lbs. elbow macaroni, cooked and drained

In a 12-quart or larger kettle, cook beef, onion and celery until beef loses redness; drain fat. Meanwhile, thoroughly blend remaining ingredients *except* cheese and macaroni in large mixing bowl; *reserve 1 quart* of this mixture. Add the *remainder* and *4 cups* cheese and the macaroni to beef mixture; blend well. Pour into *2* (12 × 20 × 1-inch) baking pans. Top with *reserved* tomato paste mixture and *remaining* cheese. Bake at 375°F 35 minutes. Makes 50 servings.

Vegetarian Lasagne

You will never miss the meat

	1	large onion, chopped
	2	cloves garlic, minced
45 ml	3	Tablesp. pure vegetable oil
225 g	½	lb. mushrooms, sliced
375 ml	1½	cups water
340 g	2	(6-oz.) or 1 (12-oz.) can Hunt's Tomato Paste
5 ml	1	teasp. _each_: salt and sugar
3 ml	½	teasp. _each_: basil and oregano
1 ml	¼	teasp. pepper
560 g	2	(10-oz.) pkgs. frozen chopped spinach, thawed and pressed dry
340 g	12	ozs. lasagne noodles, cooked and drained
450 g	1	lb. ricotta cheese
450 g	1	lb. mozzarella cheese, thinly sliced
125 ml	½	cup grated Parmesan cheese

In a large skillet, sauté onion and garlic in oil until limp. Add mushrooms; cook 2 to 3 minutes until tender. Stir in water, Hunt's Tomato Paste and seasonings; cover and simmer 5 minutes. Stir in spinach. Arrange _half_ the cooked noodles in greased 9 × 13 × 2-inch baking pan. Top with _half_ the spinach mixture, _half_ the ricotta and _half_ the mozzarella. Repeat layers, ending with mozzarella. Sprinkle with grated Parmesan. Bake, uncovered, at 350°F 30 to 40 minutes. Let stand 10 minutes before cutting. Makes 12 servings.

Porcupine Meatballs

One of our most popular recipes

2700 g	6	lbs. extra-lean ground beef
750 ml	3	cups uncooked rice
375 ml	1½	cups chopped onion
15 ml	1	Tablesp. salt
4 ml	¾	teasp. pepper
1020 g	3	(12-oz.) cans Hunt's Tomato Paste
2000 ml	2	qts. water

In a bowl, mix beef, rice, onion, salt and pepper. Form into 100 (1½-inch) meatballs. Arrange in 3 (9 × 13 × 2-inch) pans. In a large bowl, thoroughly blend Hunt's Tomato Paste and water. Pour over meatballs; cover; bake at 375°F 1 hour. Makes 25 servings.

Old-Fashioned Chili

This is the kind they brag about in Texas

900 g	2	lbs. boneless lean beef, cut in ½-inch cubes
500 ml	2	cups water
	1	beef bouillon cube
410 g	1	(14½-oz.) can Hunt's Whole Tomatoes
340 g	2	(6-oz.) or 1 (12-oz.) can Hunt's Tomato Paste
	2	cloves garlic, crushed
15 ml	1	Tablesp. chili powder
3 ml	½	teasp. oregano
	1	pinch ground cumin (optional)
30 ml	2	Tablesp. pure vegetable oil
30 ml	2	Tablesp. flour
1680 g	2	(1-lb. 14-oz.) cans small red, pinto or kidney beans, undrained

In a kettle or Dutch oven, bring meat, water and bouillon cube to boil; skim. Simmer, covered, 1 hour. Add whole tomatoes, Hunt's Tomato Paste, garlic, chili powder, oregano and cumin; mix thoroughly. Simmer 30 to 45 minutes longer or until meat is tender. Meanwhile, blend oil and flour until smooth; mix with beans. Add to chili mixture; simmer, *uncovered*, stirring occasionally, until very hot and thickened. Makes (3 quarts) 12 servings.

Buckets of Barbecue Sauce

Marvelous basting sauce

1020 g	3	(12-oz.) cans Hunt's Tomato Paste
1500 ml	1½	qts. water
500 ml	2	cups finely chopped onion
250 ml	1	cup molasses
125 ml	½	cup brown sugar, packed
60 ml	¼	cup Worcestershire
60 ml	¼	cup vinegar
15 ml	1	Tablesp. dry mustard
10 ml	2	teasp. salt
.5 ml	⅛	teasp. liquid smoke (optional)

In a Dutch oven, blend all ingredients thoroughly. Bring to boil; simmer, uncovered, 10 minutes. Makes about 3 quarts sauce, enough for 25 pounds of ribs, 100 pieces of chicken or 50 hamburgers.

To save time . . . . Prepare a whole recipe of barbecue sauce and freeze in meal-size portions for later use.

Tamale Pie

Popular casserole, multiplied for a crowd

		Water
625 ml	2½	cups cornmeal
		Chili powder
		Salt
900 g	2	lbs. lean ground beef
500 ml	2	cups chopped onion
500 ml	2	cups chopped green pepper
60 ml	¼	cup pure vegetable oil
340 g	2	(6-oz.) or 1 (12-oz.) can Hunt's Tomato Paste
256 g	4	(2¼-oz.) cans sliced ripe olives, drained
500 ml	2	cups shredded jack cheese

Bring *5 cups* water to a boil in a large kettle or Dutch oven; gradually add cornmeal, stirring constantly; cook until thick. Add *1 teaspoon* chili powder and *2 teaspoons* salt. Spread evenly over bottom of 12 × 20 × 2-inch baking pan.* Brown beef, onion and green pepper in oil in large skillet or Dutch oven; drain fat. Thoroughly blend in Hunt's Tomato Paste, 2½ *cups* water, olives, *2 tablespoons* chili powder and 1½ *teaspoons* salt. Spoon evenly over cornmeal mixture. Top with shredded cheese. Bake at 350°F for 35 to 50 minutes. Makes about 30 servings.

* Or use 2 (9 × 13 × 2-inch) baking pans.

Potluck Chicken

Pepper rings and cheese dress this up

3375 g	3	(2½-lb.) frying chickens, cut up
		Garlic salt
		Pepper
170 g	1	(6-oz.) can Hunt's Tomato Paste
298 g	1	(10½-oz.) can chicken broth
250 ml	1	cup water
5 ml	1	teasp. oregano
340 g	12	ozs. mozzarella or Swiss cheese, sliced
	3	small green peppers, cut into rings

Sprinkle chicken with garlic salt and pepper. Place, skin side up, in 2 (9 × 13 × 2-inch) baking dishes. Bake, uncovered, at 375°F 45 minutes. In a bowl, combine Hunt's Tomato Paste with chicken broth, water and oregano; pour over chicken. On each piece of chicken, place a slice of cheese and a green pepper ring. Bake 30 minutes longer or until chicken is tender. Makes 12 servings.

Baked Beans 'n Bacon

Tastes like they baked all day

225 g	9	slices bacon (about ½ lb.), cut in small pieces
250 ml	1	cup chopped onion
170 g	1	(6-oz.) can Hunt's Tomato Paste
170 ml	⅔	cup dark brown sugar, packed
1800 g	4	(16-oz.) cans Boston-style baked beans
85 ml	⅓	cup dark molasses
30 ml	2	Tablesp. red wine vinegar
15 ml	1	Tablesp. Worcestershire
8 ml	1½	teasp. dry mustard

Brown bacon and onion in a medium skillet. Drain excess fat. Stir in Hunt's Tomato Paste and brown sugar. Combine in a 2½-quart oblong baking dish with all remaining ingredients. Mix thoroughly. Bake, uncovered, at 300°F 2½ hours. Stir occasionally. Makes 12 (¾ cup) servings.

Chicken Chipotle

Perfect casual buffet dish

1000 ml	4	cups chopped cooked chicken
60 ml	¼	cup each: slivered almonds, sliced ripe olives and raisins
340 g	2	(6-oz.) or 1 (12-oz.) can Hunt's Tomato Paste
500 ml	2	cups chicken broth
60 ml	¼	cup vinegar
45 ml	3	Tablesp. brown sugar, packed
	2	cloves garlic, minced
10 ml	2	teasp. paprika
5 ml	1	teasp. hickory-flavored salt
1 ml	¼	teasp. crushed red pepper
	2	dozen corn tortillas
750 ml	3	cups shredded Monterey Jack cheese

In a medium bowl, lightly toss chicken with almonds, olives and raisins; set aside. In another bowl, thoroughly blend remaining ingredients *except* tortillas and cheese. Arrange alternate layers of tortillas, chicken mixture, tortillas, sauce mixture, tortillas and cheese in a greased 9 × 13 × 2-inch baking pan, ending with a layer of cheese. Bake at 375°F 30 to 35 minutes. Makes 12 servings.

Spaghetti Meat Sauce for Fifty

Everybody loves spaghetti

1800 g	4 lbs. lean ground beef
	4 large onions, chopped
	4 cloves garlic, minced
2040 g	6 (12-oz.) cans Hunt's Tomato Paste
790 g	1 (28-oz.) can Hunt's Whole Tomatoes
2500 ml	2½ quarts water
60 ml	¼ cup brown sugar
30 ml	2 Tablesp. salt
10 ml	2 teasp. each: basil and oregano

In a large kettle, lightly cook beef, onion and garlic until onion is
tender and beef loses redness; drain fat. Stir in remaining
ingredients. Simmer, *uncovered*, 1 hour, stirring occasionally.
Serve over hot cooked spaghetti. Makes 50 (rounded ½ cup)
servings.

Cooking Spaghetti for Fifty: In several deep kettles, cook 7 *pounds*
spaghetti in boiling, salted water according to label directions until
tender. Drain and serve. Makes 50 (1 cup) servings.

Baked Chili Relleno

Extra-easy version

450 g	1 lb. Cheddar cheese, shredded
450 g	1 lb. jack cheese, shredded
220 g	2 (4-oz.) cans diced green chilies
	10 eggs, separated
370 g	1 (13-oz.) can evaporated milk
30 ml	2 Tablesp. flour
5 ml	1 teasp. salt
1 ml	¼ teasp. pepper
375 ml	1½ cups Mexicana Salsa (see page 82)

Sprinkle shredded cheeses and chilies evenly over the bottoms of
2 greased 9 × 13 × 2-inch baking pans. In a large bowl, beat egg
whites to soft peaks. In another bowl, beat egg *yolks*, evaporated
milk, flour, salt and pepper. Fold egg mixtures together; spread
over cheese and chilies. Bake at 325°F 20 minutes. Spoon
Mexicana Salsa over casseroles. Bake 20 minutes longer or until a
knife inserted in the center comes out clean. Serve immediately.
Makes 16 to 20 servings.

Reach for Hunt's Tomato Paste

When You Need a Super-Saving, Super-Tasty Main Dish . . .

Everyone is just as hungry when the budget wears thin as when it's fat. Those are the times when your ingenuity and your skill as a cook get their biggest workout. These tasty, wholesome dishes can come to the rescue. Here you'll find some meatless wonders that depend on eggs or cheese for their substantial goodness, some thrift-minded specials that make a little meat taste like a lot.

Opposite: Polenta Ring-Around (see page 11

Polenta Ring-Around (Illustrated page 117)

This budget saver looks spectacular

430 ml	1¾	cups (about 8-oz. pkg.) corn muffin mix
5 ml	1	teasp. paprika
	1	egg
85 ml	⅓	cup milk
250 ml	1	cup shredded Cheddar cheese
225 g	½	lb. Italian sausage
	1	med. onion, sliced
450 g	4	zucchini (about 1 lb.), sliced
170 g	1	(6-oz.) can Hunt's Tomato Paste
250 ml	1	cup water
3 ml	½	teasp. salt
		Grated Parmesan cheese (optional)

In a bowl, combine muffin mix and paprika. Add egg and milk; stir until just mixed but still lumpy. Fold in shredded cheese. Fill greased 1-quart ring mold. Bake at 400°F 15 minutes. Meanwhile, remove sausage from casings; chop coarsely and brown in 10-inch skillet. Add onion, separated into rings, and zucchini; toss to mix. Cover; cook, stirring occasionally, until onion is limp. Add Hunt's Tomato Paste mixed with water and salt; mix gently. Cover; simmer about 10 minutes. To serve, turn out "polenta" ring on platter. Fill center with sausage mixture. Sprinkle with Parmesan, if desired. Makes 6 servings.

Beef 'n Bean Burrito

A tortilla folded around a super filling!

340 g	1	(12-oz.) can roast beef with gravy*
85 ml	⅓	cup Mexicana Salsa (see pg. 82)
575 g	1	(1-lb. 4½-oz.) can refried beans
110 g	4	ozs. sharp Cheddar cheese, shredded
	8	(7-inch) flour tortillas

In a small saucepan, combine beef and gravy with Mexicana Salsa, separating beef chunks into shreds. Heat through, stirring occasionally. In another saucepan, combine refried beans and cheese; heat through over low heat, stirring occasionally, until cheese is melted. Meanwhile, wrap tortillas in foil and warm in oven at 300°F 5 to 10 minutes. Place equal portions of meat and bean mixtures in center of each warm tortilla; fold sides and ends over to enclose filling. Serve with additional Mexicana Salsa, if desired. Makes 8 burritos.

* Or use 1½ cups shredded leftover roast beef.

Baked Swiss Strata

An economical brunch entrée

125 ml	½ cup finely chopped onion
30 ml	2 Tablesp. butter or margarine
500 ml	1 pt. cottage cheese
284 g	1 (10-oz.) pkg. frozen chopped broccoli, thawed and drained
5 ml	1 teasp. salt
3 ml	½ teasp. fines herbes
	4 eggs
170 g	1 (6-oz.) can Hunt's Tomato Paste
500 ml	2 cups water
	12 slices white bread
225 g	8 ozs. Swiss cheese, shredded

In a small skillet, sauté onion in butter until soft. Add cottage cheese, broccoli, ½ *teaspoon* salt, fines herbes and 2 eggs, well beaten. Mix well; set aside. Beat *remaining* eggs in a bowl; blend in Hunt's Tomato Paste, then water and remaining ½ *teaspoon* salt; set aside. Arrange 6 slices bread in bottom of buttered 9 x 13 x 2-inch baking dish. Add layers of *half* the cottage cheese mixture and *half* the Swiss cheese. Pour on *half* the tomato paste mixture. Repeat layers, pouring *remaining* tomato paste mixture over all. Pierce all over with meat fork; let stand 1 hour. Bake at 350°F 45 to 50 minutes. Makes 8 to 10 servings.

To save money... Use cheese and eggs in place of more expensive forms of protein for low-cost, high-nutrition meals.

Hunt's Macaroni and Cheese

Two kinds of cheese make this special

225 g	8 ozs. shell macaroni, cooked and drained
250 ml	1 cup cottage cheese
250 ml	1 cup shredded Cheddar cheese
60 ml	¼ cup chopped parsley
60 ml	¼ cup finely chopped onion
5 ml	1 teasp. salt
170 g	1 (6-oz.) can Hunt's Tomato Paste
250 ml	1 cup water

In a large bowl, combine macaroni with cottage cheese, *half* the Cheddar cheese, parsley, onion and salt. Thoroughly mix Hunt's Tomato Paste and water in a bowl; add to macaroni mixture; blend well. Turn into lightly greased 1½-quart casserole; sprinkle with *remaining* Cheddar cheese. Bake at 375°F 20 to 30 minutes. Makes 4 servings.

Split Pea Chowder

Serve half, freeze half

450 g	1 lb. green split peas
2000 ml	2 qts. water
225 g	½ lb. ham scraps, coarsely chopped, or 1 leftover meaty ham bone
	1 small onion, chopped
250 ml	1 cup chopped celery
	1 carrot, sliced
170 g	1 (6-oz.) can Hunt's Tomato Paste
13 ml	2½ teasp. seasoned salt
1 ml	¼ teasp. pepper
1 ml	¼ teasp. ground thyme
	1 bay leaf
298 g	1 (10½-oz.) can chicken broth

In a Dutch oven or kettle, combine all ingredients *except* chicken broth; mix thoroughly. Bring to boil; lower heat and simmer, covered, 1½ to 2 hours until peas are tender. Stir occasionally. Remove bay leaf; stir in chicken broth and heat through. Makes 8 (1½ cup) servings.

For the family of four: Empty *half* of chowder into foil-lined bowl; freeze. Remove frozen soup, wrap and store in freezer to serve later.

Skillet-Quick Stuffed Peppers

Short cut to an old favorite

225 g	½ lb. skinless pork sausage links, coarsely chopped
	1 small onion, chopped
375 ml	1½ cups quick-cooking rice
	Salt
170 g	1 (6-oz.) can Hunt's Tomato Paste
	Water
	3 medium green peppers
3 ml	½ teasp. basil
250 ml	1 cup shredded sharp Cheddar cheese

In a 12-inch skillet, brown sausage and onion together until onion is soft. Stir in rice, *½ teaspoon* salt, ½ *can* of Hunt's Tomato Paste and *2 cups* water; mix thoroughly. Bring to boil, stirring. Cover; remove from heat; let stand 7 minutes. Cut peppers in half lengthwise; remove and discard stems and seeds. Immerse in pan of *boiling* water; cover; let stand 5 minutes. Drain thoroughly. Fill with sausage and rice mixture. Add *remaining* tomato paste, basil, ½ *teaspoon* salt and *1 cup* water to skillet; mix. Arrange stuffed pepper halves in sauce; top each with cheese. Cover; simmer 10 to 15 minutes. Baste once or twice. Makes 4 to 6 servings.

Minute Steak Stew

Ready in no time at all

450 g	1 lb. cube or minute steaks
45 ml	3 Tablesp. butter or margarine
750 ml	3 cups frozen mixed vegetables
410 g	1 (14½-oz.) can whole potatoes, drained and halved
30 ml	2 Tablesp. finely chopped onion
5 ml	1 teasp. salt
.5 ml	⅛ teasp. pepper
3 ml	½ teasp. bouquet garni (optional)
28 g	1 (about 1-oz.) env. brown gravy mix
375 ml	1½ cups water
170 g	1 (6-oz.) can Hunt's Tomato Paste

Cut steaks into ½ × 2-inch strips. Brown in 12-inch skillet in butter. Add frozen mixed vegetables, potatoes and onion; toss with meat. Sprinkle with salt, pepper and bouquet garni. Blend gravy mix with water and Hunt's Tomato Paste in small bowl. Stir into skillet mixture. Cover; simmer 15 minutes, stirring occasionally. Makes 4 to 6 servings.

Sauced Seashells Maritime

New way with thrifty tuna

195 g	1 (7-oz.) can tuna
125 ml	½ cup chopped onion
250 ml	1 cup chopped celery
	1 clove garlic, minced
170 g	1 (6-oz.) can Hunt's Tomato Paste
250 ml	1 cup water
	1 chicken bouillon cube
3 ml	½ teasp. each: oregano, basil and salt
225 g	8 ozs. small shell macaroni, cooked and drained
15 ml	1 Tablesp. butter
60 ml	¼ cup grated Parmesan cheese
	Minced parsley (optional)

Drain oil from tuna into 10-inch skillet; reserve tuna. Add onion, celery and garlic to skillet; sauté. stirring until onion is soft. Add Hunt's Tomato Paste, water, bouillon cube, oregano. basil and salt; mix thoroughly. Cover; simmer 10 minutes. Add tuna; mix gently; heat through. Toss hot cooked macaroni with butter and Parmesan. Spoon tuna mixture over macaroni. Top with parsley, if desired. Makes 4 to 6 servings.

Easy Patio Kabobs

Cook indoors or out

170 g	1	(6-oz.) can Hunt's Tomato Paste
225 g	1	(8-oz.) can pineapple chunks
60 ml	¼	cup lemon juice or vinegar
30 ml	2	Tablesp. molasses
15 ml	1	Tablesp. prepared mustard
15 ml	1	Tablesp. Worcestershire
5 ml	1	teasp. salt
340 g	1	(12-oz.) can luncheon meat
	8	(10-inch) skewers
450 g	1	(1-lb.) can yams, cut in chunks
	1	bunch green onions, tops removed
	1	green pepper, cut in 1-inch squares

In a small bowl, combine Hunt's Tomato Paste, *juice* from pineapple and *next 5* ingredients. Mix thoroughly; set aside. Cut luncheon meat into 1-inch cubes. Arrange on skewers alternately with pieces of yam, green onions, green pepper and pineapple. Place in large shallow baking dish. Pour tomato paste mixture over all, turning kabobs to coat thoroughly. Marinate 1 to 2 hours. Cook 10 to 15 minutes in broiler or over outdoor grill 3 inches from source of heat. Turn and baste once or twice. Makes 4 to 6 servings.

Danish Meatball Appetizers

Bite-size flavor delights

375 ml	1½	cups soft bread crumbs
	1	egg
250 ml	1	cup applesauce
170 g	1	(6-oz.) can Hunt's Tomato Paste
5 ml	1	teasp. salt
3 ml	½	teasp. nutmeg
.5 ml	⅛	teasp. pepper
450 g	1	lb. ground beef
225 g	½	lb. bulk pork sausage
60 ml	¼	cup minced onion
180 ml	¾	cup water
60 ml	¼	cup white wine or orange juice
15 ml	1	Tablesp. brown sugar, packed

In a bowl, combine bread crumbs, egg, *½ cup* applesauce, *2 tablespoons* Hunt's Tomato Paste and seasonings; mix well. Add ground beef, sausage and onion; blend thoroughly. Form into bite-size meatballs. Arrange on large shallow baking or jelly roll pan. Bake at 450°F 20 minutes. Meanwhile, in a saucepan, combine *remaining* applesauce and tomato paste, water, wine and brown sugar; mix. Simmer 5 minutes. Add meatballs. Serve warm. Makes 40 meatballs.

ALL ABOUT HUNT'S TOMATO PASTE

When you use Hunt's Tomato Paste in your good cooking, you have the satisfaction of knowing that you're using the best, a truly thick, rich tomato paste. Hunt's has fine, smooth, deep-down tomato flavor that comes from using high-quality, vine-ripened tomatoes. Then Hunt's slow-simmers the tomatoes into rich, thick tomato paste, so that you can get that "just-right" flavor and thickness without cooking for hours—so tomato paste can save you time. Another thing that's good to know: Hunt's Tomato Paste is unseasoned, except for a trace of salt. You can flavor and season as you like, create dishes that are mild and mellow or hot and spicy.

Because Hunt's Tomato Paste is a rich concentrate, it offers you more. Tomato paste lets *you* adjust the thickness of your sauce to suit *your* taste by adding as much or as little liquid as you want. No other tomato product gives you as much flexibility. A little tomato paste goes a long way; a tablespoon or two added to soups, gravy or bottled salad dressing will really perk up the flavor. Just one 6-ounce can of tomato paste contains about the same amount of tomato goodness as two 8-ounce cans of tomato sauce or a 15½-ounce jar of prepared spaghetti sauce—so tomato paste can save you money. It can even save space on your pantry shelf.

This book has acquainted you with the variety of recipes in which Hunt's Tomato Paste plays a starring role. But that is only the beginning. Branch out. Go on to try the fine flavor and thick, rich goodness of Hunt's Tomato Paste in your own dishes, in those from other cookbooks, in recipes shared with you by your relatives, your neighbors, your friends. The following chart will show you how to use tomato paste in place of other forms of tomato called for in recipes.

You can use:	When a recipe calls for:
1 (6-oz.) can Hunt's Tomato Paste plus 1 cup water	1 (15-oz.) can tomato sauce 2 lbs. fresh tomatoes, cooked 2 cups tomato puree 1 (1-lb.) can whole or stewed tomatoes

"Enjoy"—that's the wish of the authors of this book, the Hunt-Wesson Kitchens staff:

Nancy Freeberg
Carolyn Avelino
Delois Brown
Martha Johnson
Kitty O'Connell

Index

Authors / Hunt-Wesson Kitchen Staff
Cover design / Doug Kennedy
Photography / Tom Kelley
Coordination / Janice Cooperstein